THOMAS MORE AND CANTERBURY

BENEATH THIS FLOOR
IS THE VAULT OF THE
ROPER FAMILY IN WHICH
IS INTERRED THE HEAD OF
SIR THOMAS MORE
OF ILLUSTRIOUS MEMORY
SOMETIME LORD CHANCELLOR
OF ENGLAND WHO WAS
BEHEADED ON TOWER HILL
6TH JULY 1535

ECCLESIA ANGLICANA LIBERA SIT

AD 1932

Marble Memorial to Sir Thomas More in the pavement of the St Nicholas (Roper) Chapel in St Dunstan's Church, Canterbury. The design is by Lawrence Turner.

THOMAS MORE

AND CANTERBURY

*Selected addresses for the annual
Commemoration of Thomas More
in the Church of St Dunstan
Canterbury*

Edited by

HUGH OLIVER ALBIN

DOWNSIDE ABBEY
BATH

Dedicated to the

AMICI THOMÆ MORI

wherever they may be.

————

The publication of this book
has been made possible by a grant from
The Parochial Church Council of Saint Dunstan's,
Canterbury and the Jane Hodge Foundation.

Downside Abbey
Stratton on the Fosse
Bath, England, BA3 4RH

British Library Cataloguing in Publication Data:
A catalogue record for this book is available from
The British Library.

ISBN   1-898663-00-9

Typeset at Downside Abbey, Bath.
Printed and bound by Hobbs the Printers, Southampton

CONTENTS

FOREWORD

When Thomas More was beheaded on Tower Hill on 6th July 1535, though his body was laid to rest in the Church of St. Peter ad Vinculum, in the Tower of London, his head was brought by his daughter Margaret to the Church of St Dunstan in Canterbury, the parish church of the Roper family, into which Margaret had married. That his head should lie not half a mile from the place where another Thomas suffered martyrdom for his resistance to another dictator King, another Henry, is both appropriate and significant, though the significance is not just that both saints challenged the invasion of the State into what they perceived as the realm of God. Today, both Becket and More — in a way in which not all saints do — seem to transcend the differences and the divisions into which, since their day, Christendom and Christianity itself have fallen. In the late twentieth-century world both have an appeal which makes them 'ecumenical' saints, and, in the case of Thomas More, the present work makes this abundantly plain. It is a collection of sermons and addresses delivered in St. Dunstan's, Canterbury, at the annual ecumenical service to commemorate the martyrdom of Thomas More. Of the contributors, some are Anglican, some Roman Catholic, some Free Church; two were Archbishops, many are lay; some are historians, others lawyers; two are Australian. Though there is such a variety of approach, there is a minimum of repetition, and as a complete whole, the book gives a picture in depth of the saint's character, outlook and significance.

I warmly commend this book, for it is not only a valuable contribution to the growing corpus of scholarly work on Thomas More, but it also reveals why More has become so powerful a figure today. As one of the contributors has so perceptively put it: 'And so More chose martyrdom: to be a martyr of conscience. It is this that we love and admire in him today and which makes him both a Catholic and a Protestant in the truest sense.'

John A. Simpson
Dean of Canterbury

vi

PREFACE

The following addresses were given over the years 1971-1992 in St Dunstan's Church, Canterbury. In 1971 I inaugurated an annual commemorative address in the context of a religious service to mark the association of the church with Thomas More. The saint's head rests within the Roper vault in the church so that the latter has become, over the years, somewhat of a pilgrimage centre for devotees of More.

A further association with Canterbury is, of course, William Roper who had a manor house close to the church and who had married Margaret More, the eldest daughter of Sir Thomas. The More and Roper families must have made many visits from time to time to Canterbury and St Dunstan's.

Through the years St Dunstan's has taken a keen interest in ecumenism. The annual commemorative service was, and still is, a means of bringing together Christians from different churches. I and my wife have been privileged in meeting personally and acting as hosts to those who have contributed the addresses for this book.

I am pleased that the present Vicar of St Dunstan's — the Reverend Maurice Worgan — and his Parochial Church Council have encouraged me to collate the addresses and to try to form them into a book. This has not been easy for, with so many writers involved — all writing on a common theme — there must, inevitably, be a certain duplication. However, with the help of my publisher, Dom Charles Fitzgerald-Lombard, I hope we have given some kind of unity and direction to the book. I am grateful to all those who have helped us in our task and especially the contributors and the Parochial Church Council of St Dunstan's for their practical help.

The addresses speak to us of Thomas More from many different viewpoints. As the Abbé Germain Marc'hadour gave us two addresses on separate occasions, I decided that his contribution on More and Canterbury deserved the extra space and, indeed, needed this to preserve the unity of his contribution.

It only remains for me to thank the Abbot and Community of Downside Abbey for their help in the production of this book. I trust it will be received as a further contribution to More studies.

'Panorama'   Hugh O. Albin
Coombe Cross   *formerly Vicar of*
Bovey Tracey   *St Dunstan's, Canterbury*
S.Devon   All Saints 1993

vii

CHRONOLOGY

1474   John More of London marries Agnes Graunger.

1477/8 6/7 February: Thomas More born in Milk Street, Cripplegate. Exact date and year uncertain.

1490   Thomas as a page to Archbishop Morton at Lambeth.

1492   Thomas More enters Oxford University.

1494   Leaves Oxford to begin his legal career at New Inn.

1496   Admitted to Lincoln's Inn, his father's Inn of Court.

1499   Meets with Erasmus.

1501   Called to the Bar. Tests vocation to the priesthood.

1504   Marries Joanna (Jane), the eldest daughter of Sir John Colt M.P. of Netherhall, Roydon, Essex. He lives at The Old Barge, Bucklersbury, Walbrook.

1505   Margaret, More's eldest daughter, is born.

1505/6 Erasmus stays as guest at Bucklersbury.

1506   Elizabeth, More's second daughter, is born.

1507   Cicely, his third daughter, is born.

1509   Henry VIII succeeds as King (d.1547). More's only son John is born.

1510   More as under-sheriff of London (until 1518)

1511   Jane More, his wife, dies at 23 years of age. More marries Alice Middleton (b. circa 1471) widow of John Middleton, mercer, of London.

1515   First embassy mission to Flanders. *Utopia* begun in Antwerp (published at Louvain in 1516).

1517   More's second embassy mission, to Calais (until 1518). Member of the King's Council.

1521   Receives knighthood and becomes Undertreasurer. Henry VIII receives the title of *Fidei defensor*. Margaret More marries William Roper (2 July).

1523   More becomes Speaker of the House of Commons.

1524   Chancellor of the royal duchy of Lancaster.

1526   Hans Holbein is a guest in More's household.

1529   More succeeds Cardinal Wolsey as Lord Chancellor. Resigns in 1532 (16 May).

1534   He is imprisoned for refusing to sign the Act of Succession (17 April).

1535   Beheaded for high treason (6 July).

1935   Pius XI canonises John Fisher and Thomas More.

I ARCHDEACON BERNARD CLINTON PAWLEY

Born in Portsmouth in 1911, the son of a naval officer, Bernard Pawley was educated at Portsmouth Grammar School and Wadham College, Oxford (BA 1933; MA 1936). He trained for the ministry at Wells Theological College and held curacies at Stoke on Trent and Leeds Parish Church. He became an Army chaplain in 1940, was captured in the desert at the battle of the Gazzala Line and was POW in Italy and Germany 1942-44 (mentioned in despatches). Appointed Vicar of Elland, Yorks 1945-55; Clerical Diocesan Secretary, Ely 1955-59; Canon Residentiary Ely Cathedral 1959-70; Archbishop of Canterbury's representative at the Vatican 1961-65; Canon Residentiary and Chancellor of St Paul's 1970-72; Archdeacon of Canterbury 1972-81. He was the author of Looking at the Vatican Council *(SCM Press 1962); editor of* The Second Vatican Council: Studies by eight Anglican Observers *(OUP 1967) and co-author with Margaret Pawley of* Rome and Canterbury through Four Centuries *(Mowbrays 1974/81).*

It is a considerable honour for me to be here to help celebrate the memory of a great Englishman, a fellow citizen of London, Saint and Martyr, Thomas More. We are here partly, though not primarily, to commemorate one of the shameful deeds of English history, his execution. And we are here also because we hope by our prayers and by our common action, not only to see that this kind of event does not happen again, but to try and bring about the conditions in which the unity of the Church may be restored.

I divide what I have to say into three parts: The first, of course, must turn to the words of the Lord Himself; to the sacred scriptures, to see how they speak to us. What do you make, in these circumstances, of St Matthew 23:29? Here is a warning:

> Alas for you... You build up the tombs of the prophets and embellish the monuments of the saints and you say 'If we had been alive in our father's time, we should never have taken part with them in the murder of the prophets'. So you acknowledge that you are the sons of the men who killed the prophets.

1

What about that? Does that hit home? Are we still doing or allowing to be done any of the happenings that led up to this tragedy? It is not so much the individual details, or even the persons with which we are most concerned, but the general principles. We must remember that we are thinking of the days before the Church of England as a separate body came into existence under Queen Elizabeth. We share a common guilt, as the Roman Catholic and the Church of England now together explore the activities of Henry VIII *Defensor Fidei*.

But still, after four hundred years, we Anglicans have not shaken off the shackles of state control, at least in the provinces of Canterbury and York. That must be the chief line of penitence, in my view, that we of the Church of England should be following this evening. Reforms in the papacy overdue in St Thomas More's day, are still not complete, though Paul VI has proved a reforming pope. And I imagine that our brethren of the Roman Catholic Church will be reflecting that although some of the other reforms which St Thomas More prayed and worked for, were brought about at last by the Second Vatican Council, there are still some after four centuries which are not achieved.

And here we must be careful not to idealise too greatly the character of St Thomas More himself. He was a liberal reformer, and a disciple of the new knowledge of the time. Yet he did not blench at the prospect of the burning of heretics and he still conceived some of his doctrinal attitudes in terms of the late middle ages which were not then long passed. Had he been alive today, it is probable that he would have been numbered among the reformers such as Hans Küng,[1] Karl Rahner[2] and Henri de Lubac.[3] He died in protest against the blasphemy of the King as Head of the Church; a title which the Church of England has never subsequently allowed; and in that sense a martyr for the papacy. A papacy clearly that he would have hoped would have reformed itself more than it has done. He was in many respects an enigmatic man; though a disciple, as I have said, of the 'new knowledge' that was part of the Renaissance, he misunderstood some of its learning and some of his fellow reformers; he was a little harsh, to say the least of it, to the Maid of Kent.

So we all need, at a time like this, to remember our Saviour's words: at all costs to try not to feel self-righteous; never to try to claim the saints as our own contentiously; never to use them as foibles to play off against our fellow-Christians, as we all have done in the past with the blessed martyrs of Smithfield and Tyburn. The first part of our thinking, therefore, can be of penitence. *Kyrie eleison.*

Secondly, we can give thanks for the immensely long way we have been able to come together in the cause of restoring the unity of Christendom. Only a few years ago, this joint celebration would not have been possible. *Thanks be to God.*

Thirdly, we must consider the implications of the foregoing factors in our common search for unity. Let us take a lead from Thomas More's chief literary work, the *Utopia.* For there, as you know (in spite of the fact that he was a zealous contender for the truth as he saw it), in *Utopia* he realised that there must be a kind of pluriformity in man's apprehension of God. And in the ideal state there was to be no place for religious intolerance. He writes:

> It is a monstrous thing that man should set upon man to oblige him to seek God by force in a way which is not his own.

That kind of sentiment he would doubtless hand on to us today. We have suffered much among the churches, on all sides, from intolerance, but we have now travelled together a long time and found what St Paul would have called 'a more excellent way'. The Second Vatican Council has crossed out of its canons the old belief that error has no rights, and has left behind it a whole new school of thought which is prepared to recognize that the one truth can, under certain circumstances, be apprehended or expressed in different ways. The Inquisition has become the Holy Office and now the Congregation for the Teaching of the Faith.

Pope Paul VI himself has said that we must expect a certain pluralism in the expression of religious truth. He has encouraged our representatives[4] to explore further the belief that doctrines themselves can be graded in importance as between: those essential for salvation; essential for full union; essential for ecclesiastical intercommunion and those which, while claiming a general allegiance, are optional, rather than essential; all this without compromising the promise of the Holy Spirit to lead us into all truth. (That promise did not extend to detailed formulations of truth).

There are many people these days who are speaking and thinking like this. They are carrying on the work of Thomas More and his nearest colleagues Colet[5] and Erasmus[6]. They are picking up again the promptings of the Holy Spirit to the Church which, four hundred years ago, were stifled by the insensitivity of popes and the brash ambition of kings.

The token stone which is being flown tomorrow to Kansas City[7] will bear with it the good wishes of us all. Let us hope that none of the dark shadows of English Church history and controversy accompany the gift. In the United States, dialogue between the churches has gone along faster than it has been able to do in England, because they are not weighed down as heavily as we are by the legacy of former centuries. Pray God, therefore, that it will be a sign of our common determination to bury the bitter memories of the English past and to commemorate those pure spirits who breathed the clearer ecumenical air of today, four hundred years before their time. Perhaps in ecclesiastical affairs, if God's good will, it may become possible for the churches to call in the new world to redress the balance of the old.

NOTES

1. Radical Swiss Roman Catholic theologian, for many years Professor at the University of Tübingen.
2. German Jesuit theologian.
3. French Jesuit theologian.
4. Members of ARCIC — Anglican-Roman Catholic International Commission, set up by Pope Paul VI and Archbishop Ramsey in 1966, all of whom are determined that the Church should be in contact with the laity and measure up to the challenges of educated humanism.
5. John Colet (1466-1519), Dean of St Paul's, protagonist of the new learning.
6. Desiderius Erasmus (1466-1536), Humanist scholar in the Netherlands, who visited More in England.
7. On 7 July 1971, the Vicar of St Dunstan's, Canterbury, the Revd Hugh Albin, flew to Kansas City with a piece of stone from the flooring of the Roper Chapel, for presentation to the Roman Catholic church of St Thomas More.

4

II MISS ANNE ROPER, J.P.,M.B.E.,M.A.,F.S.A.

A graduate of University College, Cardiff, Anne Roper spent much of her life sorting through the New Romney archives exploring the history of Kent Churches. She was the driving force behind many local history projects chiefly connected with Romney Marsh and South East Kent. During World War II she was an Army Welfare Officer and was awarded the M.B.E. in 1944. A member of the Oxford University panel of extra-mural lecturers, she gave many lectures on Marsh History, Kentish Inns, the Cinque Ports and Smuggling. In 1948 she was appointed a delegate to the First World Council of Churches held in Amsterdam and elected to attend the second Council in the United States. A Vice-President of the Kent Archaeological Society for many years, she became the first woman President of the Association of Men of Kent and Kentish Men. For nearly 20 years she was Honorary Archivist to the Corporation of Hythe, a J.P. for 19 years, a Churchwarden for 50 years and a Fellow of the Society of Antiquaries. In 1984 she received the Lambeth Degree of Master of Arts of the University of Oxford conferred upon her by the then Archbishop of Canterbury. Anne Roper was Lord of the Manor of Eastbridge, one of the Manors of Romney Marsh. She took a great interest in Thomas More studies with special interest in research into the Roper family.

Some forty years ago, the late Dame Elizabeth Wordsworth wrote: 'There are certain periods as well as certain personalities in history which appeal to us in an exceptional way. Among the former the sixteenth century is undoubtedly pre-eminent.'

Few of us would disagree with this statement. That particular century was halfway between the mediaeval and the modern world and was preceded by the invention of printing and the discovery of America. It really was what Shakespeare said of his own time, a 'growing age'.

The personality of exceptional appeal was of that distinguished and lovable statesman Sir Thomas More, one of the figures of abiding interest in English history. No century could boast of a group of such remarkable men as were his friends. They included Erasmus, the great biblical critic and scholar and one of the pioneers of the Reformation. Then

5

there was Thomas Linacre, the founder of the Royal College of Physicians in 1518; Dean Colet, the founder of St Paul's School; William Warham, the Archbishop of Canterbury and the famous painter, Holbein.

Thomas More was the son of John More and his wife, Agnes, and was born in the house where his parents were then living in Milk Street, Cheapside. His father was a well-known lawyer in the City of London and was Judge of the Common Pleas. Later on he became Judge of the King's Bench and was knighted. Their first offspring was their daughter Joan and their second child Thomas was born on 7th February, 1477. Before Thomas's mother died, two more children had been born. They were a devoted and happy family.

Under his father's influence, Thomas was destined to study law and was educated at one of the City's two best schools, St Anthony's in Threadneedle Street endowed by Henry VI; the other school was St Thomas Acons, which later became the Mercer School.

It is interesting to recall how children were educated in those days. They learned by hearing what the master said and then they would go over it in their minds at home. This method fostered a good memory which Thomas More enjoyed to the end of his days as well as the good foundation in Latin he had acquired.

His father followed the usual custom of sending his son to serve in one of the great houses of the day. He was wise and fortunate in the choice he made that Thomas should enter the service of John Morton, Archbishop of Canterbury and Lord Chancellor of England. By training Morton was a scholar, a lawyer and a churchman and by experience a diplomat and statesman. He now held the greatest offices in Church and State and was respected as the most powerful man in England and as a loyal servant of Henry VII.

The Archbishop's Manor House at Lambeth stood in beautiful surroundings with a view across the Thames to the Royal Palace of Westminster and the Abbey. In the Archbishop's house Thomas More was given an orthodox religious training and taught that spirit of reverence for authority and for the precepts of the Church which he never lost. He began to understand the terrible social evils which he described so pointedly in his Utopia and he felt that deep sympathy with the poor and oppressed which became one of the guiding motives of his life. Thomas felt for the Archbishop a lasting admiration and gratitude.

Through the Archbishop's interest, Thomas was sent to Oxford where he spent two years developing his command of Latin and studying very thoroughly formal logic. His father then brought him back to London to study common law. In February 1496, he was admitted to Lincoln's Inn and five years later he became 'an utter barrister', that is, a full member of the profession. He had a prodigious capacity for work and apart from his study and practice of the law, he read avidly from the Scriptures, the Church Fathers and tried his hand in literary fields including drama and poetry.

His parents had now moved to the Barge at Bucklersbury near Walbrook. It was quite a large house built of stone and timber with many gardens. Although bowing to his father's decision that he should become a lawyer, he tested his vocation to the priesthood and lived for four years in the Carthusian monastery adjoining Lincoln's Inn sharing in the monks' life. However, although attracted to Holy Orders, he decided he would best serve God and his fellow men as a lay Christian.

In 1505 Thomas married Joanna (Jane) Colt, the eldest daughter of an Essex gentleman farmer. She was quite young and with little schooling. But Thomas soon made her a competent hostess for his non-English visitors such as the Dutch humanist, Erasmus, who later was given permanent rooms in the Barge. It was to the Barge that Thomas brought his wife after their marriage and she died there in 1511. More never discontinued his custom of early rising, prolonged prayer, fasting and wearing a hair shirt. God always remained the very centre of his life.

Henry VIII's accession in 1509 brought Erasmus back to England and he stayed at the Barge. Here he wrote his Praise of Folly. In 1510 More was appointed one of the two Under-Sheriff's of London, the 'packhorses of the City Government'. It was not for long for in 1518 he resigned as Under-Sheriff to be fully in the King's service. In this year 1518, he bought the lease of Crosby Hall in Bishopsgate. Crosby Hall was an historic house with a fine hall built in 1466 by

Sir John Crosby, a grocer and woolman and a Sheriff of London. The hall was 87 feet long and 38 feet high. The 15th Century oak roof was divided into eight bays by arched trusses resting on old carved stone corbels, the whole lofty and majestic and on the west side a row of fine Gothic windows with a splendid circular window. Perhaps the most notable feature was the Oriel window with stone mullions and transome and stone vaulting with a boss bearing the crest and helm of Sir John Crosby. In the spandrels of the great Tudor fireplace of Reigate stone was to be seen the ram, symbolic of Sir John's association with the woollen trade.

Crosby Hall with its unique mediaeval design was where the Duke of Gloucester, afterwards Richard III, lodged after he had conveyed his innocent nephews to the tower and meditated on their murder. However, More was now very anxious to get away to the real peace of the countryside and he decided to build a house adjacent to the Thames at Chelsea. As soon as it was ready, he sold the lease of Crosby Hall to Antonio Bonvisi. The house at Chelsea was a large and comfortable home. Among his treasures here was a heart of amber, in which a fly was imprisoned, a gift from his friend Cuthbert Tunstall, Bishop of London and later of Durham, an emblem of friendship which he said could not fly away nor perish.

Though his position obliged More to keep many servants yet he would have no idle retainers in his household. Dicing and cards were strictly forbidden. Those who attended him as Lord Chancellor were expected to occupy their leisure with gardening, music or books. When he was at home on Sundays, he attended regularly his parish church (with all his household) — this was Chelsea Old Church. His household at Chelsea was a happy one and it was here that Holbein painted the delightful group of the More family.

More had begun his famous 'Utopia' during the leisure hours of his mission to Flanders. Its reception exceeded all that More could have hoped. It was translated (from the Latin) into French, Italian, Dutch and German before it was into English. The earliest edition appeared at Louvain at the end of 1516. The breadth of view and depth of insight of this speculative essay contrasting an ideal society with the evils of the existing one gained for the author a reputation for being far in advance of his own age, in social and economic thought. Many of the questions raised are of perennial interest — the distribution of wealth, the problem of unemployment, depopulation of country districts, the equable division of labour, equality of opportunity, the position of women, education and marriage, punishment of crime; no subject was too great and none too small from the highest problems of moral philosophy down to a proposal for the incubation of chickens. 'The chykens assone as they become oute of the shel follow men and women insteade of the hennes.'

More's deep interest in the new learning found expression in the education of his children. He chose for them the best available teachers in divinity, classics, astronomy and music. He himself supervised and shared their studies. He had the gift of turning the driest subject into a delightful pastime. 'It surely must have been of More's children', says Mr See-bohm, 'of whom Erasmus speaks, as learning the Greek alphabet by shooting with their bows and arrows at the letters.'

More's ideas on education were well expressed in a letter to William Gunnell, tutor to his children, which makes clear his principle that the aim of education should be not an accumulation of knowledge but the development of a sincere and modest character. He writes:

> I was particularly pleased to observe that Elizabeth shows as much gentleness and self-command in her mother's absence, as would be possible were she present. Let her understand that this pleases me more than all possible letters from anyone.
>
> Though I esteem learning joined to virtue more than all the treasures of Kings, yet renown for learning, when it is not united with a good life, is no more than distinguished infamy. This would be especially the case in a woman, and since learning in women is a new thing, and a reproach to the slothfulness of men, many will be ready to attack it and will impute to learning what is really the fault of nature ...
>
> I have often begged you, my dearest Gunnell, and my wife, but also all my friends, to warn my children to avoid the precipices of pride and to walk in the pleasant meadows of modesty. Let them put virtue in the first place, learning in

9

the second, and esteem most in their studies whatever teaches them piety towards God, charity to all and Christian humility in themselves.

If it be true that the soil of a woman's brain is naturally poor, and more apt to bear bracken than corn, (a saying by which many keep women from study) then so much the more, for that reason, should a woman's mind be diligently cultivated and the defect redressed by industry. This was the opinion of the ancients, of those who were the wisest and most holy. Do you, then, my most learned Gunnell, of your goodness make it your care that my girls learn well the works of those holy men.

In later years the children remembered the quaint and homely sayings with which their father was wont to encourage them on the Heavenward road. Such as:

It is no mastery for you children to go to Heaven, for everybody giveth you good counsel, everybody giveth you good example. You see virtue rewarded and vice punished so that you are carried up to Heaven even by the chins.

We may not look at our pleasures to go to Heaven in feather beds; it is not the way, for Our Lord himself went thither with great pain and by many tribulations... The servant may not look to be in better case than his Master.

I have endeavoured to give some picture of Sir Thomas More, the *Man*. Not the lawyer, or the statesman, or Speaker of the House or the Lord Chancellor. All this has passed into our history books. He showed to all men of his time the duty man owes to God. Be the temptation of power, worldly honour, wealth, even the family, ever so great, a man must choose the *Spirit*. The King's servant must be God's servant first.

More has been called the Man for all Seasons; he has become the man of all nations and it has been suggested the patron saint of Europe. Sir Winston Churchill's tribute in his *History of the English People* says succinctly — 'More stood forth as the defender of all that was finest in the mediaeval outlook.'

On the life-size statue of Sir Thomas More outside Chelsea Old Church are the three words that sum up his life — Statesman, Scholar, Saint.

10

III The Reverend Hugh Oliver Albin, M.A.,B.D.

Born in Northern Ireland, the Reverend Hugh O.Albin was a Senior Exhibitioner, Foundation Scholar and Gold Medalist of Trinity College, Dublin, and member of the Senate of Dublin University. A former Rector of Moston, Manchester, and Vicar of Bethersden, Kent, he became Vicar of St Dunstan's with Holy Cross, Canterbury in 1970. During his incumbency the two new windows in the Roper Chapel were inserted and the new church hall was built. He was Vicar of St Dunstan's until his retirement in 1988.

As founder of the Friends of St Dunstan's and of the annual Thomas More Commemorative Services, he formed national and international links with Thomas More scholars and churches, chiefly in France, Germany and the United States and is a contributor to the journal Moreana. *He now lives in retirement with his wife, Betty, in Bovey Tracey, South Devon.*

In the first part of my address this evening I have given you reminiscences of some of the personalities who graced this annual Commemoration Service over the years 1971 - 1992. Now, in the second part I hope to share with you some of my thoughts on Thomas More. I find him somewhat unusual in being both a brilliant scholar and such a complete man. More seemed to excel in almost everything. People are attracted to him because of his love of fellowship. He was a great family man. As the years went by his family increased, for as his children married he could not bear to be parted from them nor they from him, with the result that he made room for them so that they and their children could make their home with him. He enjoyed sitting at table with his family or entertaining his friends, showing his sparkling wit and interspersing the conversation with the new learning of the Renaissance. The great Dutch scholar Erasmus was only one of many entertained at his table.

His all-round merit is seen moreover in his impressive business sense. Indeed I often think of him as our first European — a pioneer — for in 1515 he was sent to Flanders to conduct important negotiations on behalf of both the Crown and the City. The trade in English wool and Flemish cloth was of great importance to the merchants of both countries and great hardship was felt when political causes interrupted the export of English wool. It is said that More crossed the Channel at least fourteen times for King and Country. If he were living today, whilst approving of a closer co-operation among European countries, he would not approve of Europe's becoming isolated and being tempted to exploit poorer nations. He would see all nations on the basis of an equality. To that extent perhaps, he was a Universalist. In this European work, More was a great success.

It was not long however, before More's wide learning, his shrewd common sense, his interest in astronomy, his love of music and not least, as I have mentioned, his ready wit all commended him to King Henry. It is thought that life at Court did not really attract him, yet as Erasmus tells us, 'the King could not rest until he dragged More to his Court'.

Although forced to work in the City, he really loved the peace of the countryside, moving from Crosby Hall in the City to Chelsea, where he had a spacious house and garden. His house was full of interesting and beautiful things, including his valuable books. He loved his garden full of lovely flowers and blossoming fruit trees. He had a special affection for the herb 'rosemary' and allowed it to run all over his garden walks, not only because his bees loved it but also because it was for him the herb sacred to friendship and to remembrance.

Thomas More was a man of prayer and meditation. Every morning he would go with his children for prayer in his Chapel to say with them certain psalms and collects. When far from home, his thoughts were never far from his family. Like so many of the saints before and after him More always put God at the centre of his heart and life. He had the saint's vision of being able to rise above the changes and chances of this fleeting world. On his return from Cambrai in 1529, when he learned of the disastrous fire to his farm buildings and the loss of the whole year's corn, he wrote to Dame Alice his wife: 'Saving God's pleasure, it were great pity of so much good corn lost, yet since it hath liked Him to send us such a chance, we must and are bounden not only to be content but also to be glad of His visitation ... I pray you be of good cheer and thank God both for what He hath given us and for what He hath taken from us and for what he hath left us.'

But what about More's serious thought? A few brief words, then, on God, the Church, Authority and Conscience. As a philosopher he would have subscribed to the principle of 'Seeing all things in God.' For More everything of significance declared the glory of God. Like many others of his day, God's existence was taken by him as a first principle. It never occurred to the religious minds of his day that they were all really guilty of the logical error of *petitio principii* or begging of the question, that is, assuming what one wants to prove.

Perhaps this kind of assumption explains why, for More, there was always a 'mystery' in God. God is revealed to man rather than proved by reason. So Philosophy for him, as for many others, was to be seen as the handmaid of religion and revelation. God is chiefly known through His Power and Fatherhood; also through his Love and Goodness.

Furthermore, More in his 'Dialogue concerning Tyndale' gives us, with other matters, what I consider is an interesting account of human nature and shows us how human beings can come to experience the reality of God.

He points out that man is 'naturally selfish'. He tells us that we are more conscious of ourselves as being the centre of reality rather than of God being so. Indeed, consciousness of God is almost non-existent. How, then, can man ever come to an experience of God's existence — an experience not so much rational as one that is felt and is more real?

We are told that the answer is through Prayer. By using prayer and all the other 'available means of grace' man can find God gradually, as a reality. Man's 'natural selfishness' also begins to disappear. He is conscious now of being a 'different' self and his relationship to God is now real and meaningful.

Applying the concept of God to the concept of the Church, More saw the Church as a kind of 'Icon' of God, a symbol or image or revelation of the Divine. Accepting the Church was tantamount to accepting God's existence. We should also relate things to God automatically. Civilisation, for example, would crumble unless we presuppose a Divine Plan for

13

History. More saw the Church as the existing Catholic
Church. He said, 'it is the clergy, lay folk and all who do
stand together and agree in the confession of one true
Catholic faith.'

The Church must always be visible and well known. It had
a history — from the time of Christ to the present. It was
witnessed to by the 'Fathers', by its unity of thought and so
on. But the heretics, in contrast, showed a chaotic diversity.
They proved a threat to the unity of the Church. Miracles
were also a distinguishing visible feature of the true Church.
More also acknowledged, however, an 'invisible' or secret
element in the Church. This was the Spirit of God within the
Church leading it into all truth. The Church was a continu-
ation of the Incarnation through history. It was one family,
the household of the faith and one body. The unity of the
Church meant much to More. But his idea of the Church as
God's household - implying a diversity of persons with
differing attitudes of mind and yet one under God - is an
interesting ecumenical idea. The source of this idea of the
Church as God's Household is Psalm 67/68:6, which More
paraphrases as 'the Holy Ghost maketh all of one mind in the
house of God.'[1] It is also used in St Paul's letters to the
Galatians (6:10) and to the Ephesians (2:19-22). More
develops the idea when he retorts to Robert Barnes's 'What
the Church is' in Book 8 of *The Confutation of Tyndale's
Answer.*

More regarded the concept of Authority as resting in the
whole 'corpus' of Christian people. His doctrine of 'common
consent' was derived from this concept. Professor Richard
Marius comments that More very nearly converted this
doctrine of 'common consent' into an infallible authority for
custom - a doctrine much criticised by the Reformers. More
thus believed that any religious practice generally performed
or any doctrine generally believed by the Christian community derives from Divine Authority because of its acceptance
by the Church as a whole. Where there is uncertainty, a
General Council of the Church should then be appealed to as
representative of all Christian people. More never regarded
the Papal office, for example, as superior to the authority of

a General Council of the Church. Do we not see here the seeds of the modern principle of Collegiality?

Furthermore, the importance of the Authority of the Church is seen when we compare this with the Authority of the Scriptures. Here More crossed swords with the Reformers. For More contended that in point of time the Church came first, so much so that the Scriptures not only owed their existence to the Church but even their interpretation. In this respect More was following his mentor St Augustine. Richard Marius and others point out that there are two important scriptural texts which for More under-gird the authority of the Catholic Church and these are John 16.13 'However, when He, the Spirit of truth is come, He will guide you into all truth' and Matthew 28.20 'And lo, I am with you always even unto the end of the world.'

It is interesting to note that the Petrine formula does not figure in this particular context. Perhaps this is consistent with More's emphasis on Authority as resting on Christian people and Councils (see above). If so, I would suggest that More was also following Apostolic Tradition as there is reasonable evidence to show that local Bishops in the early church were 'chosen by all the people' and then consecrated by the other Bishops as early as the second century A.D. (See Hippolytus *Apostolic Tradition*.)

Conscience for More must first be informed, fed by knowledge and prayer. It must also listen to reason. The decisive judgement must then be left to the individual who has done all this preparatory work. Only the decree of a General Council or the clear expression of the 'common faith' of the universal Church could override conscience. Conscience is also separate from the issues of right and wrong. For one's conscience may not be right. It could be in error. Yet if one feels one would otherwise be acting against God's law, then one must obey Conscience. This is how More felt in the matter of the Pope's Supremacy as against Henry's. The great objective questions of what is right or wrong, however, are never simple. In this context, only 'Time [itself] trieth truth' and until it does we mortals have to wrestle with what is right or wrong in the present.

The great issue of More's Conscience is still an issue. Conscience has already and will in the future involve many in the question of women priests in the ministry of the Church. Will a decree of a General Council or Synod today override individual Conscience in matters of faith and morals, or do we fall back on a Conscience which will not believe what it cannot believe? More also connects Conscience with Salvation. Regarding the Act of Supremacy he writes in a 3 June 1535 letter to his daughter Margaret: 'For if it so were that my conscience gave me against the statutes (wherein how my mind giveth me I make no declaration), then I nothing doing nor nothing saying against the statute, it were a very hard thing to compel me to say either precisely with it against my conscience *to the loss of my soul* [italics mine], or precisely against it to the destruction of my body'.

Furthermore, allowing for a certain mystical background in More (he knew, for example, Walter Hilton's *Scale of Perfection* and recommended it in the *Confutation),* I wonder might it not also be possible to suggest that More's conscience may have had a certain extra quality of expressing *revealed truth* somewhat akin to the mystic's flash of insight which would have made his conscience even more authoritative because of its identification with the still small voice of God *speaking* to him through it?

It is strange that many were prepared to accept the Act of Supremacy. Did their consciences really guide them in their judgement or perhaps their reason took over and, with the purpose of marking time, they saved their earthly lives at the expense of their consciences making cowards of them all.

But More's Spirituality would not allow him to do this in spite of pressures put upon him by 'kith and kin' and his friends. I would suggest that in the end that Spirituality may have led him to see that martyrdom could have been beckoning him. Could this have been revealed to him through his conscience?

Therefore, I am inclined to agree with the sentiments expressed by Basil, Cardinal Hume, Archbishop of Westminster who, when writing the Foreword for a commemoration booklet on More and Fisher as Martyrs some years ago, wrote:

T.S.Eliot, in writing about another martyr (St Thomas à Becket) said — 'A Christian martyrdom is never an accident, for saints are not made by accident. A martyrdom is always the design of God, for His love of men, to warn them and to lead them, to bring them back to his ways.' Thomas More and John Fisher fit this truth very well. There was a design, a purpose, in their dying beyond the edification of the Catholic Christians of their day. Their sufferings and death were part of the design of God's love which provides his people with inspiration and leadership in times of weakness.

In this subject of Conscience I believe that another great English Roman Catholic, John Henry Cardinal Newman, may later have been influenced by More. For Newman in his remarkable letter to the Duke of Norfolk showed us how important Conscience was in life. The Cardinal was very courageous when he wrote, 'If I had to drink a toast I would give a toast to the Pope and Conscience but Conscience first.' Newman continued, furthermore, that Conscience instructs and governs as the aboriginal Vicar of Christ.[2] Let us note also More's words to the Solicitor General, Sir Richard Rich, 'Your Conscience will save you and my Conscience will save me'. It could be said that More died for the Unity of the Church, obeying a Conscience which governs and obeying the Truth as he saw it before God, through his Conscience.

Finally, when in 1969 the remarkably lifelike statue of Sir Thomas More was unveiled outside his old Parish Church at Chelsea, the then Archbishop of Canterbury, Michael Ramsey, was moved to say that July 6 was the most stirring and memorable day in history. Describing More as Scholar, Saint and Social Reformer, the Archbishop claimed that his significance stood out for all time, for More was the King's good servant but God's first. May I say that I believe that is still his message for today, a message of priorities which the world should heed. Cardinal Heenan, in his speech on the same occasion, pictured the man for all seasons as a man for all nations. The Cardinal stated that 'it was not his martyrdom that mattered but his holiness. More's main purpose in life was to develop his friendship with Our Lord. Men do not become saints on the scaffold any more than they do on their death beds.'

So, in Thomas More's words 'Give me Thy Grace, good Lord, to set the world at naught,' and 'busily to labour to love Thee.' May I suggest that, when you and I can make that prayer our own, then we shall be as close to the heart and mind of Thomas More as we can ever hope to be in this life.

NOTES

1. Psalm 67.7 is the Vulgate numbering. The Hebrew numbering is 68.6. It is interesting to note that whilst some modern Bible translations do not speak so much of unanimity as of solitariness and the need for togetherness yet the Prayer Book comes closer to the Catholic tradition and More's. See also CW6 p.191/20 — 'A Dialogue concerning Heresies'. Note also that 'unanimes' is the word which occurs in the earliest Latin versions. St Cyprian interprets the phrase 'unanimes in domo' in the same way as More and Bede in his Ecclesiastical History 2.2 states that St Augustine brought the Conference of Bishops and teachers to an end at Augustine's Oak by saying — 'Let us ask our Lord who makes men to be of one mind in His Fathers House to grant us a sign from heaven and show us which tradition is to be followed …'

2. The revelatory factor which I am suggesting may have been a feature of More's Conscience is, I believe, given some weight by what Cardinal Newman writes regarding Conscience in his letter to the Duke of Norfolk saying — 'Conscience is a messenger from Him, who speaks to us behind a veil… Conscience is the aboriginal Vicar of Christ, a *prophet* (italics mine) in its informations, a monarch in its peremptoriness, a priest in its blessings and anathemas, and, even though the eternal priesthood throughout the Church could cease to be, in it (conscience) the sacerdotal principle would remain and would have a sway'.

IV THE REVEREND PROFESSOR E. GORDON RUPP,

M.A.,D.D.,F.B.A.

A Fellow of Emmanuel and Fitzwilliam Colleges in Cambridge and King's College, London, Gordon Rupp was the holder of doctorates in Divinity from Cambridge, Aberdeen and Paris. During the war years he served as a Methodist minister and later became a tutor at Richmond College and then a lecturer in Divinity at Cambridge. He was the first Professor of Church History at Manchester University in 1956. In 1967 he was appointed Principal of Wesley House, Cambridge, and subsequently Dixie Professor of Ecclesiastical History in the University. Among his published books are: The Righteousness of God; Patterns of Reformation; Just Men *and* Thomas More, the King's Good Servant *(Collins). Like Thomas More, the late Professor was a Londoner and we are told that he worked in his early career in a merchant bank in the City, a short distance from the home of Thomas More.*

> Then the Lord asked Satan — Have you considered my servant Job? You will find no one like him on earth, a man of blameless and upright life, who fears God and sets his face against wrongdoing. You incited me to ruin him without a cause — but his integrity is unshaken.

If anybody had asked us where we were going, on our way here, we must have given an ancient answer. We were going on pilgrimage to Canterbury, the remains of a holy, blissful martyr for to seek. We are here because 'beneath this floor.. is interred the head of Sir Thomas More, of illustrious memory'. A man whose life was so many sided, a character so complex that in recent years scholars have debated 'Which was the real Thomas More?' You might think this place of a skull could hardly supply the answer. For a skull is the point of anonymity, where we all become faceless men. You remember how Hamlet took up such a skull:

19

> This skull had a tongue in it and could sing once.
> It might be — the pate of a politician, one that could circumvent God, might it not?
> Or of a courtier — who could say — 'Good morrow, sweet Lord, how dost thou, sweet lord?'
> Or why may not that be the skull of a lawyer — where be his quiddities now, his quillets, his cases, his tenures — and his tricks?
> A jester — where be your gibes now?
> Your gambols, your songs —
> Your flashes of merriment that were wont to set the table in a roar — not one now to mock your grinning.

Thomas More was all these — a politician, Member of Parliament and Speaker of the House of Commons — a courtier — a trusted ambassador who signed peace treaties — a lawyer — Lord Chancellor of England — the man remembered for his merry tales, whom Henry VIII loved for his wit, a kind of Lord High Jester.

But Thomas More played other roles — it is important that he was a Londoner. Shakespeare when he wrote the opening of the *Book of Thomas More* chose an up to date place to start — a riot in the streets of London, a riot against immigrants caused by skinheads — On that Evil May day 1517 when

> out of Pauls churchyard came three hundred — they ran plump through St Nicholas Shambles and at St Martin's gate they met Sir Thomas More and other, desiring them to go home to their lodging — and almost brought them to a stay but the people threw out stones and battes and hurt diverse persons but still they threw out bricks and hot water, then they rushed through the doors of St Martins and spoiled all they found, and left few houses unspoiled

How modern, we must think, the violence — the bricks and bombs — boiling water instead of petrol — the hurt of innocent bystanders — the looting. But there in the centre Thomas More, talking, skilfully pleading — almost winning so that when it was all over the citizens chose him their spokesman to plead for mercy from the King. Then there is More the scholar, the friend of Erasmus, himself the author of marvellous writings — his study of Richard III perhaps best of all — and his classic *Utopia*, a work mankind will not willingly let die.

And More, like St Joan in the play, in love with religion. As a student he lived among the Carthusians and seems to have been drawn to share their vocation. Professor Elton finds this the explanation of some of More's baffling ambiguities — and sees him as a man drawn to the life of contemplation, but forced by his own inner struggles to go into the world, to find peace only at the very last in his cell in the Tower of London. There is truth here. More did not wear his hair shirt for purely ornamental purposes. But in the world, in his family, and in the service of his king and country he had not missed his vocation. I have met people like that, what we might call 'parsons *manqué*' and they have been rather sad people. But More recalls Wordsworth's Happy Warrior

> The generous spirit who when brought
> Among the tasks of real life hath wrought,
> upon the plan that pleased his childish thought.

And then, the lawyer. This was his trade, his skilled mastery, where he spent most of his time and earned most of his money. Even though his father was a judge, it was not influence but merit that took him right to the top of his profession. He had everything going for him, wit, eloquence, fairness, compassion; was without avarice and was incorruptible. He knew how to plead a case, and how to refrain even from good words. Margaret Roper married into a great legal family, and his other daughters married lawyers.

And he was a King's servant, of the Privy Council, to whom men murmured 'Yes, Minister!' And he was the King's friend, not just the tame humanist which princes liked to show off to visitors, but almost the only man Henry could bear to talk with after dinner — whose jokes could smile away the fret of the day, or who would take him on the roof to show the stars and explain the wonders of the heavens. And *Defender of the Faith*: part of the team captained by Henry which included the Queen and her chaplains and John Fisher, who waged warfare with their pens against the heretics who were imperilling the souls of Christian men. And although More was a layman he wrote more manfully than them all, treatise after treatise in which all his wit and eloquence and learning were displayed — a kind of super G.K.Chesterton and C.S.Lewis rolled into one. And he not only wrote but took charge of investigation of these heretics.

There is a problem here for some of us, not to be swept under the carpet. I have spent long hours in the quietness of this church trying to reckon with it. The other day an evangelical friend of mine from Australia made a pilgrimage to Norwich. He wanted to see the Lollard's Pit where on a sunny day in August 1531 they burned a rather gentle, Cambridge don — the one Hugh Latimer called 'little saint Bilney'. But the only thing More had to say for him was that he 'burned well and worthily'. But if this was a blind spot it was one which More shared with most of mediaeval christendom, the tradition of a thousand years that those who were perverse in their beliefs must be bad and evil men. And with More as with most of us, blind spots and insights belong together. He was not wrong in thinking that the Catholic faith is of all causes the one most worth fighting and dying for.

And there was his home — his household, for it included his four children, the in-laws, and eleven grandchildren — as we see that family in the famous painting — the ladies each holding a book, for the history of the higher education of women in this country cannot leave out More's schooling of his daughters. There they sit, in a great stillness of affection, in the great house at Chelsea. Here is Sir Thomas More when two thirds of his life was gone. For until 1530, there was nothing to make More consider the picture in the Old Testament of a great and honoured judge in the time of his affluence, and the devastating question — 'Doth Job fear God for nought?'

Yet within three years he had been stripped of his honours and his wealth, torn from his family, and left alone, a sick and ageing man, a prisoner in the Tower. He had not changed one whit. But the world had broken up. The divorce between Henry VIII and Catherine of Aragon, the break with Rome, the claim by Henry to be Supreme head of the Church in England. More nearly escaped. Everybody knew what he thought about the divorce, and we shall never know how involved he was with the little party of the Queen's servants. He had told the King his view, and Henry was content to leave him alone and employ him about other business. But the administering of the oath, accepting the new title, brought a crisis and when most members of the establishment were falling over themselves to show their loyalty, John Fisher and Thomas More were exceptions so eminent they could not possibly be ignored.

Fisher was a theologian, and like many theologians may have talked too much and too freely. But More was a lawyer. He was by temperament an enigmatic man — his little jokes and his humour were in some sense a defence mechanism guarding an inner privacy. Some of you know the famous novel by Andre Maurois — *The Silences of Colonel Bramble* the officer in the first world war who puffed away at his pipe and said nothing, whose silences were the most significant thing about him. The silence of Thomas More is at the heart of his tragedy. He would give nothing away. He pleaded reasons of conscience, but he would not say what those reasons were. He would not give them to Thomas Cromwell, he would not even give them to his daughter, and in fact I believe he died without giving them to anybody. And so there were the letters he would not write or receive, the books he set aside unopened: the statements he would not pen, the oaths he would not swear. It was the silences which baffled, frustrated and in the end infuriated the King. It was a skilful defence but it was also a dangerous one. For it laid him open to the charge of being mute of malice. Just once did he lower his guard and flashed out a devastating retort to Cromwell — "I will not meddle in such matters, for I am fully determined to serve God and to think upon His Passion, and my passage out of the world". It was an almost contemptuous dismissal of all the values of Henry's world and it was included in the True Bill of his indictment — where two of the four points against him were this silence.

It nearly came off, but it failed to save him. There is a striking modern parallel which you may read in Michael Balfour's fine life of Count Helmuth von Moltke, a distinguished Lutheran lawyer arrested in the aftermath of the

Hitler Bomb Plot of 1944. He too took refuge in silence — he pleaded that he had done nothing and written nothing. And at the end of the outrageous travesty of a trial before his hideous execution the Judge wrote across his papers — 'He did not only think!'.

And so to his last role, Thomas More Prisoner of Conscience

> In my conscience, [he said] this was one of the cases in which I was bounden that I should not obey my prince... in my conscience the truth seemed to me to be on the other side — wherein I had not informed my conscience neither suddenly or lightly but by long leisure and diligent search for the matter I leave every man in his own conscience and me thinketh that in good faith every man should leave me to mine.

But More's conscience was not just a private matter. It became public in its implicit challenge to all the rest.

In the Tower More told Margaret a splendid story about a bunch of northerners who came up to London and who somehow got empanelled on a London jury, to try a Londoner. Well of course, they agreed on the verdict of 'Guilty'! — except one little man who said and did nothing at all until they came to vote. His name was 'Company' — we should perhaps say 'Coompany' — and he defended himself for voting against the rest on the ground that if he went against his conscience he might have to forsake their 'coompany' for hell, which is where he would go for leaving his conscience to follow theirs. It goes to the heart of Thomas More. Conscience we sometimes say, makes cowards of us all. But there is a long succession of prisoners from Micaiah the son of Imlah to little Master 'Coompany' and Thomas More and Solzhenitsyn's comrades who say that conscience may make heroes of us all.

In the last weeks in the Tower he was a weak man and could sometimes hardly hold a pen. His last major writing, his Dialogue of Comfort against Tribulation, bears marks of failing powers though it has a beautiful meditation on the 91st Psalm. But those sadly err who think of this as a time of peaceful contemplation. It was a battle ground. For temptation was there to the very last to yield to the pressures of his friends and of his family. When, months before he had cried out 'Son Roper, the field is won!' he had indeed won a victory and made a great decision, which was a turning point. But the fight was still on. In his marginal notes to his beloved copy of the Psalms there is one word which occurs at least forty times — the word 'Demons' — that is he marked all those passages where the soul is assaulted by deadly foes, human enemies as well as the forces of darkness. If we want an image of what went on in that cell, we might turn to Matthias Grunewald's great and tremendous picture of the Temptations of Saint Antony — where the saint had been beaten to the ground and attacked by a whole posse of devils, one of which is biting his hand which is clinging to his prayer book — his life line — the jugular vein of the soul, which is faith. But he knew where to turn, to look to the Passion of Christ, and to writing out the story of Gethsemane which is all about the temptations of Christ but also about Thomas More. 'A martyr', said T.S.Eliot, 'is never an accident'. And neither is a saint. And so here More came together, found wholeness, found his complete integrity:

> "Hast thou considered my servant Job?
> You incited me to ruin him without a
> cause but his integrity is *unshaken...*"

And More might have replied with the words later in that poem:

> I know that my vindicator lives
> And that he will rise last to speak in court
> And I shall discern my witness standing at my side
> And see my defending counsel even God himself
> Whom I shall see with mine own eyes
> And not another.

I have sometimes wondered if I would have canonized Thomas More, but I have no doubts at all about his daughter. Her letters reveal the real Thomas More.

25

> Mine own good father,
> Father what think you hath been our experience since your departing from us? Surely the experience we have had of your life past and godly conversations and virtuous example and a surety not only of the continuance of the same but also a great increase by the goodness of our Lord to the great rest and gladness of your heart devoid of all earthly dregs and garnished with the noble vesture of heavenly virtues.

Who can forget, how she ran and burst through the ranks of Warders, brushing aside their halberds, and clung to her father and kissed him.

> Farewell my dear child and pray for me and I shall pray for you and all your friends that we may meet merrily in heaven.. I never liked your manner towards me better than when you kissed me, for I love when daughterly love and dear charity hath no leisure to look to worldly charity.

In the Old Testament there is the great story of Rizpah the daughter of Aiah, whose sons were slain by David

> And she took sackcloth and spread it out as a bed for herself on the rock from the beginning of the harvest until the rains came and fell from heaven upon their bodies. She allowed no bird to set upon them by day nor any wild beast by night.

So did Margaret Roper mourn and watch until at last she brought away that precious relic which turned the Thomas More story for us into a Canterbury tale; and made the peace of this sanctuary out of his holy silence. The place of a skull — 'which is in the Hebrew Golgotha' — the place of the Cross was also according to Christian legend the place where the skull of Adam was buried. So tonight the word comes to us all, reminding each of us that in Adam all die, and that in Christ all may be made alive.

There is one martyr among Bunyan's champions: Faithful, who was taken and done to death in Vanity Fair, after defying the taunts of the crowd with 'We buy the truth'. About his witness and his death Bunyan wrote some simple

26

lines which may be a fitting conclusion to our little pilgrimage this evening.

> The trials that these men do meet withal
> That are obedient to the heavenly call
> Are manifold, and suited to the flesh,
> And come, and come, and come again — fresh!
> That now or sometime else, we by them may
> Be taken, overcome, or cast away.
> O let the pilgrims, let the pilgrims then
> Be vigilant and quit themselves like men!

South view of St Dunstan's Church, Canterbury, showing (right)
the Exterior of the Roper Chapel.

V THE RIGHT REVEREND ALAN C. CLARK, D.D.
ROMAN CATHOLIC BISHOP OF EAST ANGLIA

*Bishop Alan Charles Clark, Roman Catholic Bishop of East Anglia,
was born at Bickley, Kent, in 1919 and ordained to the priesthood
in 1945. He obtained a Doctorate in Theology at the Gregorian
University, Rome, in 1948 and was appointed Tutor in Philosophy
at the English College, Rome (1948-53); Parish Priest, St Mary's,
Blackheath (1965-69); Auxiliary Bishop of Northampton (1969-76)
and Bishop of East Anglia (since 1976). He was Joint Chairman of
the Anglican, Roman Catholic International Commission 1969-81
and has been Chairman of the Department for Mission and Unity,
Bishops Conference of England and Wales since 1984. He was
made Freeman of the City of London in 1969.*

> He asked you for life and this you have given,
> days that will last from age to age.   (Psalm 21:4)

These words of the psalmist can serve as a key to my
reflections, which I am privileged to share with you on the
occasion of our united commemoration of the 500th Anniversary of the Birth of St Thomas More — Lord Chancellor,
Scholar, Saint and Martyr. No one, in our history, has ever
chosen to live his life with such intensity, such consistency,
as did Thomas More of Chelsea. The record of that life
shows that it was indeed a precious gift of God and that his
'days' have lasted from age to age as his memory has been
cherished and his name revered across the world, by Christian and non-Christian alike. In him, however, we encounter
the mysterious paradox at the heart of our Christian faith that
Thomas, in order to live 'from age to age', had to die - to
die precisely that his longing for life could be fulfilled.
United in baptism to the life, death and resurrection of Christ
— even as we are — he was born to die in order to live. His
very zest for life and all that it offered him in personal
reward and satisfaction — for he was a giant in his time —
could only reach its earthly culmination by the voluntary
surrender of that life in violent death. His less than sixty
years of sojourn here on earth were a preparation for his
constant company with us in our own equally limited life-

28

span. The grain of mustard seed was of exceptional power and strength; its potency to grow to an unparalleled height was detected from his earliest years — but the grain had to die.

Another great Englishman — G.K.Chesterton — says somewhere that we can look at something ninety-nine times and we are quite safe. Look at it the hundredth time and we are in grave danger of seeing it for the first time. In preparing my thoughts, which I share with you, I have not scrupled to read what others have said in their interpretation of the mind and heart of Thomas More and they will recognise what I have gained from their own meditations. I want us all, particularly myself, to see him for the hundredth time — even if it spells danger to our own convictions and may disturb their foundation. For it is not hard to savour the great mind and heart of Thomas, to be overwhelmed by the brilliance of his intellect and to rejoice in his sweet humanity.

Yet this yields no answer to the central question as to why, in obedience to his conscience, he chose to die rather than live. It is too facile to be content with an adherence to personal conscience as an adequate explanation of a decision that cost More hard. His stance is of considerable importance for our own contemporary understanding: for the word conscience has a way of being bandied round with irresponsibility and even triviality. What is historically unassailable, in the case of More, is that he died for a belief — not for a conjecture, or a well-supported opinion, or even for the irrefutable conclusion of an argument. He was unable in conscience to accept the position of his king because he *believed* in a vitally important element in the totality of Christian truth. As Nicholas Harpsfield writes of him: 'he was the first of any whatsoever laymen in England that died a martyr for the defence and preservation of the unity of the Catholic Church. And this is his special, peerless prerogative.' This comment is no boastful piece of insipid polemic but the strict historical record, highlighting the two problems which chiefly vexed More's sixteenth-century contemporaries — the relationship of national churches to the universal church, and the position of the papacy in the Catholic

29

Church. More's answer was eventually to be disclosed at his trial — highly and characteristically personal ('I do no man harm and I say none harm. I wish all men well. Why then do you push me to this point?') and reached only after much painful searching. The demands of his faith dictated the operation of his conscience, but he recognised that not only charity forbade him to dishonour the conscience of others but that a person's faith is a free act of adherence to truth and he had no power over another's freedom.

There is a danger of too much subtlety here but — and particularly at this present moment — there is also the danger of relegating matters of faith to the irrelevancies, issues that More saw as attacking the unity of the church without which disintegration and worse were inevitable, not least the loss of credibility that the fragmentation of belief inevitably provoked. I cannot subscribe to this kind of rationalistic humanism while I recognise in More's own thought and conceptions the true *rationale* of an authentic humanism. Who indeed does not?

But this question of irrelevance nags away at one's mind. By the time he was 50, More had worked out not only his personal priorities but, more importantly for us, the priorities of the world of his time. At the summit stood the need for universal peace, a preoccupation which tallies with what is at the heart of so much courageous political and social endeavour by so many good men and women of *our* time. More considered this need to override even the danger of heresy, even though he detested the distortion of truth and the incidence of error with all his heart — and has been accused by some historians of an attitude bordering on savagery. But the need for universal peace was even more important to him than 'the conclusion of the King's matter of his marriage'. One senses that to concentrate on this third priority, as has been frequently the case, is to simplify and even distort the ground of More's stand against the King. Robert Bolt wrote shrewdly that 'he (More) was a pivot of English life at a time when England was negotiating the sharpest corner in her spiritual history'. The tragedy of the last four centuries has been that the corner was not negotiated — to the loss and suffering of all.

We must be allowed our different perspectives and our different reading of history. But I would suggest that More's unflinching emphasis on the unity of the Church was no mere intellectual principle to which he adhered in the privacy of his conscience. Whatever part — and how noble the part! — his conscience played in reaching his decision, he stood freely on the firmer ground of faith. The unity of Christ's Church is the gift of the Lord of the Church, Christ himself, but its continued existence is subject to the choices of men. Thomas More saw the choices being made at the centre of government as at least putting at grave risk this fundamental constituent of the Church. Yes, the existence of the papacy, however much in need of reformation and renewal! Too many commentators seem to have skirted this area — an area of pain and search — in favour of the much more acceptable area of the primacy of conscience, whether the conscience be right or wrong by the standards of doctrinal truth.

No, More's agonizing choice is sited in a quite different area of the human spirit. More believed in the primacy of the Pope over the whole Church as one of the essential principles of its unity — be the Pope good or bad, indifferent or incompetent. What intensifies his position of faith is, paradoxically, his own uncertainty as to whether this was a divine provision or an institution of the Church acting universally for the common good of all Christians. His conclusion, however, was conspicuous for its clarity: namely, that the English Church could not, unilaterally, reject this primacy, could not, as he said, 'without the common consent of the body depart from the common head'. There could be no abiding unity — and therefore no fullness of Christian living — unless there was someone whose office it was to bind together the nations and their churches under the Holy Spirit — and with authority. As he put it so boldly: 'the Pope holdeth up all'.

We are not resurrecting old and weary polemical debates in this search to understand why More decided that in order to live to Christ he had to die. Rather, we are accepting that this attitude was not incidental to his acknowledged greatness; it was at the very heart. We would indeed be cowards to avoid the questions it raises.

I would love to hear, at this point, a great shout of joy, a fanfare of trumpets and to feel the uplifting of the human heart to God in gratitude and resolution. For St Thomas is looking at the Christian Churches taking up where, so to speak, he had to leave the arena. There are so many who have grasped the urgency of the contemporary need - the need for God, the need for prayer, the need for persevering charity. Enshrined in the response to that need is the daunting recognition that the disputes of the past require the arduous work of disentanglement. Here many grow faint-hearted or even perverse. For the credentials for engaging in this mammoth task are enduring hope and super-human humility. Real differences of teaching affecting the faith by which we are all saved must be confronted, and, where they have been, nothing but rewarding confidence in the authenticity of our task has been the result.

The imperatives of Christian unity may impose harsh burdens on the conscience, but that conscience has no consistency unless it is a freely accepted response to faith, the very opposite of compromise. Yes, we need the humility to recognise that we cannot be a light to the nations unless there is (among many other things equally or more important) some pastoral office in the Church which can bind us together in Christ. This in no way gainsays those who demand renewal, even reformation. But the area we are treading is the area of Christian faith and life, not the dimension of useful organisation. Ecumenism must not be allowed to freeze our differences. Reconciliation is achieved by personal struggle and a 'More-like' intense examination of conscience. It is my conviction that every Christian Church has undertaken, even if tentatively, this examination and that this is one of the most relevant preoccupations of everyone who believes in the unity of the Church.

So we step down from the argument and the debate and, rightly, look again together — for the hundredth time — at this great countryman of ours who has become our common possession and by his presence sealed our friendship. He would be horrified if I were to assert that his 'solution' is exempt from criticism or that he had any kind of personal infallibility in his judgement of where the Christian must stand. But neither could he accept that his conviction about the unity of the Church and its practical implications was at a different level from his faith in Jesus Christ.

This faith in Jesus is at the heart of his love of life, a life he possessed more abundantly the more — sometimes fearfully — he put it at risk. Steadily and steadfastly he entered into the mystery of the death and resurrection of his Lord. His discovery, at which he marvelled as he meditated on his Lord's Passion, was that his own love of life had no permanence until, through the alchemy of God's grace, he first loved eternal life and accepted the inexorable priorities it imposes. I would affirm, with little fear of contradiction, that he saw his own death as in some mysterious way a defence of the fullness of human life, as itself the affirmation of the integrity of the human spirit and the courage of the human heart. The cost was total. In Eliot's words, 'it cost not less than everything'. Our prayer tonight is that he will inspire us to pursue an equally noble purpose in living and so one day soon join his company in eternity with Him who is the Way, the Truth and the Life.

The Ecumenical window in the St Nicholas (Roper) Chapel.

33

VI The Abbé Germain Marc'hadour

The Abbé Germain Marc'hadour was born at Langonnet in the hills of Brittany on 16 April, 1921, being named after Bishop Germanus of Auxerre. The Breton surname Marc'hadour comes from the Latin mercator *meaning merchant. Ordained in 1944 and graduating in June 1945 at the Université Catholique de l'Ouest, Angers, he was appointed in 1952 to the Department of English at the University and becoming full Professor in 1970. The Abbé was awarded an M.A. at the University of Rennes in 1950 and in 1969 became a Docteur-ès-Lettres of the Sorbonne, his doctoral thesis being* Thomas More et la Bible *(Paris: Vrin). He has since edited More's* Supplication of Souls *(CW7, 1990) and written the introduction to* A Dialogue Concerning Heresies *(1981). Amongst his many publications are also* Saint Thomas More *(Namur, 1962) and* L'Univers de Thomas More (1477-1535) *(Paris: Vrin, 1963). Invited to be the International Secretary of the Association of the* Amici Thomae Mori *in 1962, the Abbé launched the bilingual quarterly* Moreana *(no. 1 in Sept. 1963). He was Editor up to his recent retirement. He was, and still is, a world wide traveller and lecturer in the service of Thomas More — Scholar, Saint and Martyr.*

THOMAS MORE AND CANTERBURY

In defiance of the chronological order, I will begin with More's letter of 5 July 1535, since it was written in the shadow — or should we say the glow — of the event which brings us together this evening. No sentence from More's English works is as often quoted, I suppose, as these lines:

> I cumber you, good Margaret, much, but I would be sorry if it should be any longer than tomorrow, for it is St Thomas even, and the utas [octave] of St Peter, and therefore tomorrow long I to go to God, it were a day very meet and convenient for me. [1]

Like the rest of the letter, written with a coal and unfinished, this sentence is rather unkempt, yet never unclear. The first 'it' has no antecedent, but whether it refers to the waiting or to the execution at the end of it matters little. The next 'it' refers to the date: 6 July, already rich in anniversaries [2], was significant for the martyr on two counts: a) as the Vigil of the solemnity of St Thomas Becket's translation, celebrated with pomp and fervour since 1220; the crowds, which could not go to Canterbury in mid-winter for the feast of his martyrdom, 29 December, made up for it on 7 July. As Chaucer writes in his famous Prologue to *The Canterbury Tales*, pilgrims started wending their steps in the direction of the shrine from mid April, and their flock reached its largest numbers towards early July when there was a secular fair as well as a religious feast. b) as the Octave of the feast of St Peter, that is the eighth day if one started on 29 June, *solemnitas sanctorum Petri et Pauli.* The two apostles together were the pillars which supported Rome's claim to the title of Apostolic See; and London, the birthplace of our two Thomases, emulated the Eternal City by also enjoying that double patronage: St Paul's Cathedral, and the Royal Abbey of St Peter at Westminster. The life of the capital revolved around those two poles. To this twin presence etymologists ascribe the proverbial phrase 'Rob Peter to pay Paul'.

From the Tower, while he writes, More can remember spending the nights from 13 to 17 April 1534 at the Abbey, in the custody of Abbot William Benson, one of the commissioners appointed to proffer the oath to the Act of Succession. He can remember 1 July 1535, when Westminster Hall, a familiar haunt for him and his father Judge Sir John More, was the stage for his trial. After sentence was passed, he precisely evoked each of the two apostles: Peter, to whom 'a spiritual preeminence' was granted 'by the mouth of our Saviour himself'; Paul, who, as Saul, had 'consented to the death of St Stephen, ... and yet be they now both twain holy saints in heaven, and shall continue there friends for ever'.[3]

The testimony just quoted stems from the Canterbury-born lawyer, Master William Roper. In his *Life of Sir Thomas More,* Roper quotes very seldom and sparingly from his father-in-law's writings; he searches his own memory and that is what makes his work a *memoir.* The main exception, I believe, concerns the passage I quoted from More's last

35

letter. Does he tacitly improve on it by changing 'it is St Thomas even' to 'tomorrow is St Thomas even'? Or is he copying a manuscript, perhaps the autograph, which might differ from our printed version? Anyway, the result gives us a triple *tomorrow* as if anticipating the famous triplication in *Macbeth* (V,5):

> Tomorrow, and tomorrow, and tomorrow
> Creeps in this petty pace from day to day...

Roper goes one step beyond reporting the *ipsissima verba* of More's 5 July testament of a letter. He singles out the line mentioning the double coincidence and repeats it immediately after his quotation:

> And so, upon the next morrow, being Tuesday, St Thomas' even and the utas of StPeter, in the year of our Lord one thousand five hundred thirty and five (according as he in his letter the day before had wished), early in the morning came to him Sir Thomas Pope, his singular friend, on message from the King and his Council, that he should before nine of the clock the same morning suffer death (Roper, p.100).

The echoing continues since the final utterance of the martyr is followed by this statement from his son-in-law: 'So passed Sir Thomas More out of this world to God, upon the very same day in which himself had most desired' (Roper, p.103).

Was More aware that the 1170 murder in the metropolitan cathedral had also taken place on a Tuesday? Or was there a deliberate pattern which made Tuesday 'a day very meet and convenient' for executions? At any rate it was the usual day. On Tuesday 4 May 1535 More, 'looking out of his window', beheld five priests 'as cheerfully going to their deaths as bridegrooms to their marriage' (Roper, p.80). John Fisher's decapitation also took place on Tuesday 22 June 1535, two weeks to the day before that of More. Their world was aware of days, more perhaps than ours. The Liturgy of the Hours gave each day some features of its own. More happens to mention the day of the week when he cannot remember the date; and Sir John More noted that his son

Thomas was born on a Friday, and Friday was to be More's day of silent reclusion during his Chelsea days (Roper, p.26).

A British scholar of distinction reckons that More, for all his youthful 'aspiration to the monastic life', 'showed little enthusiasm for the great Benedictine houses', but considered entering the Carthusian order.[4] That is unsupported conjecture. True, More expressed no enthusiasm for any order of monks, and he was no 'enthusiast'. The 'mixed life' of the Franciscans appealed to him as the holiest vocation.[5] But I do not recall a single line in derogation of the Benedictines. 'He was granted a corrody [allowance] at Glastonbury Abbey on the death of Edward Poxwell, 25 May 1519 (11 Henry VIII), and maintained contacts with this famous monastery at least until 1524, when he was present at the swearing in of the abbot-elect, Richard Whyting, in a small chapel at York Place.'[6] The most impressive evidence of friendly relations with St Benet's sons, of course, is the *Letter of Fraternity* sent to him and his wife on 23 April 1530 by the Prior and Chapter of Christ Church, Canterbury. The facsimile of the document was published, along with an English translation, in this very city on the 400th anniversary of More's execution [7], and a critical edition is available in *Sir Thomas More: Neue Briefe*, edited by Hubertus Schulte Herbrüggen.[8]

The *Littera fraternitatis* is worth pondering even though it remains tantalizingly unspecific. The community proclaims a special obligation to More on account of his love and goodwill. His benefactions must have been generous, since they are called *clarissimis*. He had been Lord Chancellor now for a half-year, but may have showed his *dilectio* (the word occurs twice) before that. The monks ascribe this affection to More's 'reverence for our most blessed patron St Thomas the martyr', to whom, as well of course as to Christ and Our Lady, they recommend him. Thomas and Alice More will participate spiritually in all the prayers, masses, fasts, alms and vigils of their Canterbury protégés. This shareholding is to last beyond their death : when their demise has been notified, their names will be registered for an annual obit to mark the anniversary (called 'the year's mind' in Early Tudor England), and recommended to all the cloisters in the kingdom, 'as is the custom'.

No allusion is made to the date, 23 April, the feast of St George. Given the year, I wonder if the bond between More and Christ Church was not created or reinforced in 1529, when he wrote the *Supplication of Souls*. In this book published twice during the weeks preceding More's elevation to the chancellorship, the inmates of purgatory refute the allegations made by Simon Fish in the virulent pamphlet entitled *A Supplication for the Beggars*. According to Fish, King John Lackland 'would have punished certain traitors' and among them a clerk called Stephen whom afterwards, against the king's will, the pope made bishop of Canterbury.' [9] You have recognized Stephen Langton, and probably, like myself, are not interested in the circumstances of his promotion. You connect him rather with *Magna Carta*. But More was eager to quench every spark of the fire lit by his incendiary, anticlerical colleague Fish. I can imagine him spending a few hours, perhaps a few days, at Canterbury doing some first-hand research in the monastic archives. The Souls, who are the speakers in his *Supplication*, sound quite confident in their retort:

> For neither was that Stephen ever traitor against the king, as far as ever we have heard, nor the pope none other wise made him archbishop than he made all other at that time; but the same Stephen was well and canonically chosen archbishop of Canterbury by the convent of the monks at Christ's Church in Canterbury, to whom, as the king well knew and denied it not, the election of the archbishop at that time belonged. Nor the king resisted not his election because of any treason that was laid against him, but was discontented therewith, and after that his election was passed and confirmed by the pope, he would not of long season suffer him to enjoy the bishopric, because himself had recommended another unto the monks, whom they rejected and preferred Stephen. And that this is as we tell you, and not as the beggars' proctor writeth for a false foundation of his railing, ye shall mow [be able to] perceive not only by divers chronicles, but also by divers monuments yet remaining as well of the

election and confirmation of the said archbishop, as of the long suit that after followed thereupon. (*CW7*, 129)

Excuse the long quotation. The text is important, and the even longer commentary in the Yale edition substantiates the accuracy of More's account. King John loathed Langton chiefly for his having lived in France as professor and rector of the Paris university. Innocent III loved Langton for having been his fellow-student, and made him cardinal even before recommending him as primate. The king rushed twice to Canterbury to influence the monks, and bullied them into electing his candidate, Bishop John de Gray of Norwich. The pope quashed that unfree election, and Langton was elected unanimously. John in his rage drove the whole monastery into exile (1207), hence the papal interdict laid on England. Langton waited until 1213 in the same Cistercian abbey of Pontigny which had harboured Thomas Becket forty years before. The chronicles (Matthew of Paris *et al*) bear out More's version of the crisis, as do the surviving documents, especially the forty-one letters concerning the election and its stormy aftermath. Of course many papers he may have consulted were destroyed at the time of the spoliation of the monasteries.

Stephen Langton is as inseparable from Thomas Becket as King John is from his father Henry II. John's suspicious nature feared lest Stephen, after years in Paris then Rome, should not prove a docile subject. But the Stephen he was eventually forced to admit into England and Canterbury had an easier task than his martyred predecessor. The formula which More, at his trial, quoted from *Magna Carta* [10], and which St Dunstan's church, Canterbury, has revealed to many pilgrims by carving it into stone, *ut Ecclesia anglicana libera sit*, was a perfect summary of Becket's demand, and the ground of his martyrdom. By winning freedom for the Church of England, Becket won it also prestige and prosperity, not always well used over the centuries.

Erasmus visited the almshouse just outside Canterbury on the way to London, and gave a tip to the old beggar who gave him (as also to all other pilgrims) 'the upper part of a shoe' to kiss, a relic of St Thomas. Like his companion John

Colet, he found this practice rather disgusting, yet makes it an occasion for praising the martyr:

> Good men, truly, are in every respect useful to everyone: as this saint, during his lifetime, encouraged people to holiness by his example, teaching, and exhortations, comforted the forsaken, and raised up the needy. In death his usefulness was almost greater. He built this very wealthy church [*hoc locupletissimum templum* — meaning the cathedral]; he strengthened considerably the influence of the clergy throughout England. Lastly this piece of shoe supports a house of poor men. [11]

This is Ogygius speaking in a colloquy, but there is no reason to believe that More's friend did not share More's affection for his patron-saint. Erasmus visited Becket's shrine with a letter of recommendation from Archbishop William Warham, his most generous Maecenas, who had given him the living of Aldington, Kent. More was the middleman in exchanging the pension money into the currency Erasmus used wherever he was. Warham was a canon lawyer, like Becket, and had, like him, served the king as chancellor. Toward the end of his life, he steeled himself to imitate St Thomas. When the Administration threatened him with a charge of *praemunire*, he replied in terms reminiscent of Becket, vindicating 'the laws of God and Holy Church':

> And if in my case, my lords, you think to draw your swords and hew me in small pieces, ... I think it more better for me to suffer the same than, against my conscience, to confess this article to be *praemunire* for which St Thomas died. [12]

As a Frenchman, I must add that Langton's exile in France was the best preparation for the solemn translation of his predecessor's relics, which he presided over in 1220. At Sens, then a primatial see for northern France and thus a kind of counterpart to Canterbury, he saw many relics of the martyr. Enamels, reliquaries and mosaics were beginning to multiply before Langton crossed the Channel to take possession of his see. Before 1240, four French cathedrals had told Becket's story in sequences of stained glass: twentyfive scenes in Chartres, which had had John of Salisbury as bishop, thirteen in Sens, eight in Angers, cradle of the Plantagenet dynasty, and six in Coutances, a Norman city rich in English connections. [13]

WITNESSES TO MANGER AND CROSS

I return to Erasmus's colloquy *Peregrinatio religionis ergo* because it was written by More's closest friend, and because it is the finest literary document about Canterbury on the eve of the Reformation. Ogygius the pilgrim has only one interlocutor, Menedemus, 'the stay at home', as the Greek name means. Menedemus is a married man, he commutes between his house and his shop, which leaves him no time to visit distant shrines. He sometimes speaks with the voice of Thomas More, not least when, after hearing of Becket's mitre and other relics, he asks: '*Nulla crux?*' '*Nullam vidi*' is Ogygius' answer (I-3, p.488). The staff shown to the pilgrims 'looked like a cane plated with silver', much like a nobler walking stick, with no cross at the top. We can understand Menedemus' question and share his surprise. In the Becket iconography of French cathedrals, prominence is given to his processional cross, the symbol of his autonomous power as head of the English Church, as well as of his readiness to shed his blood in the cause of the Redeemer, 'blood for blood' as Eliot puts it. Becket used his primatial cross as a kind of sceptre; he wielded it very visibly during his confrontation with Henry II and his own fellow-bishops.

But no less importantly the cross was the badge of English chivalry: the large red cross still at the heart of the Union Jack is that of St George, patron of England and patron of the knightly order. More must have been mindful of it when he walked to the scaffold holding in his hands a crude red cross of his own making: two pieces of wood painted red and put together by his heavy hands spoke more starkly than any finely wrought crucifix. He was being 'Sir Thomas, knight'. The symbolism survived the iconoclastic bout of early Reformation. Many holy roods were pulled down and made merry bonfires, yet the 'gentle knight' of Spencer's *Faerie Queene* is an Elizabethan St George from the very first stanza:

But on his breast a bloody cross he bore,
The dear remembrance of his dying Lord,
For whose sweet sake that glorious badge he
wore,
And dead as living ever him adored.

But solidarity with Christ is not limited to emulating his
bloody sacrifice, which is an exceptional vocation. The daily
witnessing consists in espousing his poverty. This both
Becket and More elected to do through a monastic style in
their dress, their diet and their hospitality. Care of the poor
is an essential chapter in St Benet's rule: whoever knocks at
the monastery door is welcomed as Christ in person.
Erasmus, who does not write as a tourist but as the preacher
he always was, singles out the almshouse he encountered on
his steep way from St Dunstan's towards Harbledown and
London. Here Becket's name is still a talisman for 'little old
fellows' in dire need. Erasmus' own alms to the inmate who
brings the *calceum sancti Thomae* under his nose is ungrudg-
ing. His denunciation of the absurd hoarding of precious
metal occurs in another, earlier, colloquy, the *Convivium
religiosum* of 1552. It was his first ever mention of Becket's
shrine, and he speaks through the mouth of Eusebius, 'the
pious man':

> I for one would prefer to see all that superfluity made
> available to the poor, instead of its being kept for satraps
> some day to plunder it all: *Ego malim ista, quae superflua
> sunt, elargiri in usus pauperum, quam servare satrapis
> aliquando semel omnia direpturis.*[14]

This is almost a startling prediction of the 1538 spoliation, in
which the 'satraps' of England pretended holy motives. One
of their prophets was Dr. (*quondam* Friar) Robert Barnes,
who echoes Erasmus' *Peregrinatio* only to rail at the exter-
nals and superstitions of the Catholic Church. 'You take also
to help you St Thomas of Canterbury's holy shoe', he wrote
in 1531, and More quoted that unfair sentence in his *Confutation* (*CW*8, p. 861), without bothering to comment on it.
He knew, though, that the shoe, of all relics, helped the
poor, not the monks. During the centuries of official ostra-

cism against 'Becket the traitor', Erasmus' dispassionate and discreet homage to the blissful martyr must have acted as a counterweight to Bale and Foxe. I will take one witness from the eighteenth century, the *Twenty-Two Select Colloquies out of Erasmus*, translated by Roger l'Estrange (London, 1725). The title page recommends this book for its 'representing several superstitious levities that were crept into the Church of Rome'. Yet l'Estrange is admirably faithful to his model, in full awareness that 'some will have him to be a papist in masquerade for going so far' (Preface). I repeat in his version a passage I have already quoted:

> He [Becket] comforted the friendless, assisted the needy, and if it were possible, he does more good now he is dead than he did living: he built this magnificent church, and advanced the authority of the priesthood all over England; nay, and with this very fragment of his shoe, he maintains a conventicle of poor men (pp. 49-50).

PILGRIM AND MARTYR

I have already insisted on the idea of pilgrimage, because our generation has rediscovered the spiritual significance of a certain nomadism. *Homo viator* can tread a genuine pilgrim's way as he goes the round of his daily occupations. As Goethe said, Europe was born of pilgrimages. The very title of Dr. Ramsey's *Canterbury Pilgrim* is a provocative encapsulation of that vision. To me it evokes the image of archbishops commuting between Lambeth Palace and their metropolitan cathedral, or returning to their headquarters after visits to overseas dioceses of the Anglican communion, or to the heads of sister-Churches. More, the 'stay-at-home' who loathed embassies, was a keen pilgrim, and believed in using his own feet. He defended Erasmus' scholarly wanderings by likening them to the apostolic travels of Christ, or of the missionaries, and the mendicant friars. Until his day, only a few students would come to England from the Continent, since neither Oxford nor Cambridge attained to first magnitude in the galaxy of Christendom's universities, nor was English at all useful as an international language. The only major tide across the Channel was of pilgrims.

St Thomas Becket paid for his resistance to secular encroachment with almost seven years of exile. He spent more of his episcopal time in France than in England. This gives weight to his 2 December 1170 sermon on the text of Hebrews 13:14, 'We have not here a dwelling city, but we seek the city that is to come'. I have quoted the verse in the words of Thomas More, who makes it the epigraph of his *Treatise upon the Passion*, and quotes it repeatedly.[15] More, who suffered and expressed his homesickness when royal missions kept him too long away from his family, could understand what a cruel trial it was for St Thomas Becket to see his closest relatives and his servants sharing the precariousness and the discomforts of his own exile, while his pastoral children were left fatherless.

'A Christian martyr is never an accident, for Saints are not made by accident', says the archbishop in Eliot's play.[16] Still less is martyrdom a tragedy. We may view the disgrace of a Thomas Wolsey and a Thomas Cromwell as a tragic fall, in the sense of Boccacio's *De casibus illustrium virorum*. But the death of Thomas Becket and of Thomas More is a fall only in the sense of Autumn, 'season of mellow fruitfulness', when all the seeds and blossoms of a lifetime come to full fruition. More, Erasmus says, is a remarkable extempore speaker, but the same Erasmus shows More practising the orator's skill with deliberate perseverance, so we know that the seemingly impromptu performance was the result of systematic drilling. The final test of our two martyrs was, similarly, prepared by lifetime habits of self-inflicted discipline, long vigils, austere diet, even the hairshirt. The Christmas liturgy itself blends the mysteries of joy and sorrow, links the incarnation with the stoning of St Stephen, the massacre of the Innocents, the flight of the Holy Family into Egypt, the drops of blood shed by Jesus on his eighth day when he received the name which means 'the Lord heals'. The Christian folklore of England is attuned to that painstaking spirit when, in a Christmas carol, 'good King Wenceslas' is shown honouring 'the feast of Stephen' with a generous errand to serve his Master in the guise of a stranger in need.

Thomas Becket's last sermon is eloquent by the saints he singles out. After the Mother of God, he names only two bishops, both martyrs. One, St Denys, of universal fame, is the patron of Paris, where young Becket had studied. The hill on which Denys and his companions were executed is still called Montmartre, *mons martyrum*. His feast, October 9th, a red-letter day even in the Sarum calendar, ushered in the Autumn term in both English universities. Among his own predecessors, Becket does not evoke Augustine, founder of the see, nor St Dunstan, of great national fame, but St Elphege, the good shepherd slain by pagans not in hatred of the faith, but because he would not fleece his flock to levy the money for his ransom. [17]

TRES THOMAE

Allow me to defy chronology once more by drawing on the very first biography of More that was published, as part of a sizable volume, entitled *Tres Thomae* (Douai, 1588). The author, a recusant theologian, Stapleton, presents himself as a fourth Thomas praising his two canonised patrons and his revered fellow Englishman More who, though not 'sainted' yet, was a true martyr. Stapleton speaks of the Apostle briefly, as hardly known to us beyond what the gospel says. He has more to tell about the Archbishop, thanks to letters he has discovered. The *Thomae Mori vita* is a full account of More's life and works, much of it based on firsthand records. In chapter 19, Stapleton expatiates upon the phrase 'St Thomas' Eve'. [18] His Continental readers did not know that, in the Sarum calendar, the feast of the Translation was a red-letter day, liturgically superior to the Octave of Peter and Paul, which was the only feast of 6 July in the rest of Christendom. Even Stapleton's students in the Douai Seminary may have been ignorant of the 7 July Translation, since the feast had disappeared with the desecration of the shrine in 1538, before their own birth. The Translation of St Thomas the Apostle was celebrated on 3 July, also in England, and in 1535 that feast occurred while More was awaiting execution. But 'doubting Thomas' would have provided a poor coincidence, as More treats the Apostle as a negative model, who rejected the testimony of many

45

trustworthy witnesses.[19] Being a red-letter day in England, the Translation of St Thomas Becket was celebrated already on July 6th though a vigil — at Vespers of that day; the Octave was reduced to a mere commemoration. Stapleton shows the propriety of the double evocation in More's letter, but stresses 'St Thomas' Eve':

> Why *very meet and convenient*? Because that day was the Translation of St Thomas of Canterbury — not a public holiday, yet very highly celebrated in the Church... It was therefore not without reason that Thomas More wished to be *translated* from these darknesses to light and become a martyr on the glorious Translation of his patron, St Thomas the martyr.[20]

ANOTHER TRIAD OF THOMASES

Long before *Tres Thomae* was published, another full biography of More was composed, here in Canterbury, by a Londoner like Becket and More, and an Oxford alumnus, Nicholas Harpsfield. He was born in 1519, the same year as Archbishop Grindal, the Primate whose Puritan austerity displeased Elizabeth I. He was admitted archdeacon of Canterbury on 31 March 1554, succeeding Edmund Cranmer, the married brother of Archbishop Thomas. As archdeacon, Harpsfield, in November 1554, welcomed Cardinal Pole to his cathedral with a long oration, and entertained him in his own house. On 24 March 1558 he was appointed to the living of Bishopsbourne (which was to have Richard Hooker as an incumbent in 1562). On 28 October 1558, Pole made him 'Dean of the Peculiars', that is of the parishes outside the diocese of Canterbury (thirteen in London alone) which came under the Archbishop's jurisdiction. On 1 November 1558, he became a canon of Christ Church. Sixteen days later, both Reginald Pole and Queen Mary died. For refusing the Elizabethan Uniformity, Harpsfield was deprived and spent the rest of his life in confinement, dying in London on 18 December 1575.

The Life and Death of Sir Thomas More was meant for publication, but, because of Mary Tudor's death, it remained in manuscript until 1932, when Elsie Vaughan Hitchcock, helped by R.W. Chambers, produced the authoritative edition for the Early English Text Society. She calls it 'the first serious attempt at a complete Life of More, with an account of his literary work'. Harpsfield dedicates his biography to William Roper, then also a citizen of Canterbury, and Member of Parliament for Canterbury in 1555:

> Ye shall receive, I will not say a pig of your own sow — it were too homely and swinish a term — but rather a comely and goodly garland...picked and gathered even out of your own garden...And yet we have also paid some part of the shot...We have gleaned, I trust, some good grapes...(p. 6).

It is one of those good grapes that I want to pick, without revisiting the account of More's death, where the author reproduces Roper's memoir verbatim. In his commentary, he institutes one of the parallels dear to biographers, 'craving leave of the blessed martyrs St Thomas of Dover and St Thomas of Canterbury' (p. 214) to praise More above them. Thomas of Dover 'was slain of the Frenchmen' in 1295 because 'he would not disclose to them where the jewels and treasure of the monastery was' (p. 214-215). Becket is more familiar to Harpsfield's readers, many of whom remember how, less than two decades ago, people worse than Henry II 'unshrined him, and burnt his holy bones' (p.215). The monk and the archbishop were genuine martyrs, yet Sir Thomas can boast 'a deeper cause of martyrdom' — not the possessions of a monastery, not just 'the dignity and privilege of the Church', but 'the preservation of the unity of Christ's Church' (p. 213). The parallel between Becket and More bears rereading in full:

> Howbeit, as StThomas of Canterbury and he were of one and the selfsame Christian name, and as there was great conformity in their birthplace at London, and that they were both Chancellors of the realm; and in that StThomas of Canterbury, when his troubles began, coming to the king carried his cross himself, not suffering his chaplain, or any of the bishops that offered themselves, to carry it; and in that Sir Thomas More, when his great troubles first

grew on him, carried the cross in procession himself at Chelsea, the clerk being out of the way; and that both ever after carried, though not the material cross, yet the very true cross of Christ, by tribulation, to the time and (of all) at the time of their glorious passion; and that there was a conformity in that Sir Thomas More died according to his desire on the eve of St Thomas of Canterbury; so was there great conformity in the cause of their martyrdom (p. 216).

Both, then, witnessed with their lives, and with the giving thereof, for the Church of Christ, one for its freedom, the other for its unity.

'THE WICKED WOMAN OF CANTERBURY'

Elizabeth Barton, one of those mysterious women about whom historians remain baffled and divided, must have been the most trying of More's Canterbury connections. His estimate of her veered from a measure of affectionate reverence to a very harsh dismissal. She is labelled 'the Nun of Kent' because her first trances and predictions occurred while she was in the service of Warham's steward on an estate in Aldington, the village we already encountered as the benefice granted to Erasmus by the archbishop. She was examined by the Prior and two monks of Christ Church, Canterbury, and, in 1527, admitted into the Benedictine priory of the Holy Sepulchre, Canterbury. Thenceforth she was called 'the nun of Canterbury' (by More, Rogers, p. 470), or 'a certain nun dwelling in Canterbury' (Harpsfield, p. 155). When Elizabeth, under examination by Cranmer, and then publicly both at Canterbury and in London, confessed that her visions were not genuine, and that she was puffed into a public role by the praises of learned men, More espoused the accusers' conclusion: he calls her 'the lewd nun of Canterbury' (p. 40 — 'lewd' meaning unsound and villainous in a broad way, with no reference to lechery), then 'the wicked woman of Canterbury' (p. 489).[21] In their editing of this letter for publication in More's *English Works* of 1557, his literary executors returned to the non-committal label 'the nun of Canterbury', and so does Harpsfield when

48

he quotes the letter (p. 61). No doubt they had learned a good deal about the results of questioning and torture, and would not take the nun's self-accusation at face value.

In two letters to Cromwell, during the first trimester of 1534, More documents every stage of his implication. He first heard of 'that huswife' around 1525 from the King himself, who gave him 'a roll of paper in which were written certain words...spoken in her trances' (p. 481). 'About Christmas' (1532), Richard Risby, guardian of the Franciscan Observants at Canterbury, 'lodged one night at mine house' and spoke with admiration of the nun. Notice that, though she is in a Benedictine cloister, the Franciscans are busiest promoting her; another of More's guests in this connection is also an Observant. Though now a private citizen, More practises the duty of reserve. He will not listen to anything that has to do with 'the king's matters'. He never saw Father Risby again until 23 November 1533, when the friar publicly acknowledged his complicity at Paul's Cross. Meanwhile, he had interviewed the nun at the Bridgettine house of Syon, Isleworth, upstream from his own Chelsea. She impressed him rather well and seemed to accept his counsel of discretion. He gave her 'a double ducat, and prayed her to pray for me and mine'.

Not content with oral advice, he addressed to her a letter focussing on the message 'Do not meddle with politics'. It begins 'Good Madam, and my right dearly beloved sister in our Lord God' (p. 465). I hope, More says, 'that your wisdom and the Spirit of God shall keep you from talking with any persons, specially with lay persons, of any such manner things as pertain to princes' affairs or the state of the realm' (p. 466). A copy of that letter convinced the House of Lords and the Royal *ad hoc* Commission that More's name should be removed from the list of persons attaindered for complicity, and it was. Hearing 'her own confession declared at Paul's Cross' in November 1533 revealed to him 'the evil spirit that inspired her'. He sent word to the proctor of the Charterhouse at Sheen that 'she was undoubtedly proved a false deceiving hypocrite' (p. 487).

The Administration had lost a very convenient handle to compromise him in something treasonable, yet did not quite let go of that handle, as we find in the account More gives of his appearance before the Lords at Lambeth Palace on 13 April 1534. Two members of the Commission appointed to tender the oath were Doctors of Divinity : 'my Lord of Canterbury' (p. 505), that is Thomas Cranmer, and 'my Lord of Westminster' (p. 506), namely abbot William Benson of Westminster. The other two were his fellow-lawyers, Chancellor Thomas Audley and 'Master Secretary' Thomas Cromwell. We need not reread the arguments put forth by the two divines [22], as our point is the Nun of Kent, evoked by Cromwell in connection with the King's wrath : 'For surely the King's Highness would now conceive a great suspicion against me, and think that the matter of the nun of Canterbury was all contrived by my drift. To which I said that the contrary was true and well-known' (p. 506).

More does not seem to have wanted, before the other Commissioners, to remind Cromwell of the documented correspondence he had sent him only weeks before. Nor was he taken aback by the development which made him, from a mere conniver, the master-minder of the dark plot. This letter is treated as no. 1 of the Tower writings, and yet my impression is that it was an impersonal account of the encounter with the Commission, a memorandum couched on paper during the three days More spent 'as a prisoner' (p.501) under the surveillance of the Abbot. If it was sent to Margaret (who is never named, nor is anyone addressed, nor is the letter finished or signed) after her father's incarceration (17 April), it may well not have reached its intended readers before the Nun was executed at Tyburn (20 April 1534) with her counsellors and abettors.

MORE AND 'MY LORDS OF CANTERBURY'

More's instinct, or perhaps his habit at any rate, was to respect authority as such. He defended Erasmus' *New Testament* by repeatedly pointing out that the Supreme Pontiff had approved of it. In the Hunne affair, he invoked the verdict passed by judges of the king's appointing. Cranmer was playing on that disposition when, on 13 April 1534, he urged More to dismiss his doubts about the Act of Succession, and 'take the sure way of obeying of your prince' (Rogers, p. 505). More, in the opinion of R.W. Chambers, 'was staggered that this argument should be put forward by the Primate of England, the successor of Warham and Becket'. [23] Cranmer trod that 'sure way' of obedience until 1556, when he chose to obey his conscience and disobey the queen who was then his 'Supreme Head under Christ'.

The same logic of reverence prompted More to stress the function and almost ignore its exercisers' personalities. At Lambeth, he will not see four frightened mortals, but two prelates of Mother Church, and two officers of his anointed sovereign. None of their names will appear in his memorandum. Even when he refers to Warham in writing to Cromwell, he says 'the bishop of Canterbury that then was, God assoil his soul' (Rogers, p. 481). No reverential epithets are needed for a dead person; Archbishop Bourchier in *Richard III* is often called plain *Cardinalis*, or 'the cardinal'.[24] But while ecclesiastical dignitaries are alive, More uses full titles, duly graded too, for instance 'the most reverend Father in God, the Archbishop of Canterbury' and 'the reverend Father, the Bishop of Rochester' (*CW*8, 15).

We have just encountered Cranmer as the third archbishop of Canterbury in More's life, so I will speak of him first, building on the substantial introduction (pp. 84-89) to the 1530 Fraternity Letter in Professor Schulte Herbrüggen's *Neue Briefe*. More had conferred with Dr. Cranmer before he became 'most reverend', over 'the king's great matter', and of course read the *Determinations of the Universities* edited by Cranmer in 1531 [25], a book he certainly disliked, though he showed it to the House of Commons, as the king's mouthpiece. He refused to attend the coronation of Anne on 1 June 1533, the first public event at which Cranmer, only two months consecrated, officiated in the splendour of a liturgy he had not yet simplified. Cranmer was also a member of the Commission before which More appeared to answer the charge of supporting the Nun of Kent (Harpsfield, p. 157). We have seen the two men face to face at Lambeth on 13 April 1534. On 3 June 1535, the King's Council came all the way to the Tower for a last assault on the former

Chancellor, hoping to drive him to speak his mind one way or the other.

In enumerating the five personages, Moré gives precedence to 'my Lord of Canterbury' (Rogers, p. 556). He probably never knew on earth that Cranmer, on 17 April 1534, had written to Cromwell in an attempt to save him and Fisher by suggesting that they be allowed to swear to a modified version of the oath. Cranmer puts forth motives of policy; their subscribing would influence other potential objectors. But he may also have followed his gentle nature as he is known to have pleaded for other victims. [26] Nor did Cranmer know, I suppose, that More, writing to Erasmus in June 1533 (the very month of Anne's coronation), congratulated the humanist on the fact that Warham's successor was as friendly as Warham had been, and would continue the pension (Allen, ep. 2831).

Cranmer did not go much to Canterbury, probably never as a pilgrim, though he did visit the shrine of Becket at the time of its 'disgarnishing', and we can reckon he was sincere in applauding the end of an 'abomination'. Robert Bolt dramatizes More's execution by bringing the primate on stage. On the rostrum More says to Cranmer 'I beseech your Grace, go back', and, offended, Cranmer does so. And when More says to the executioner 'You send me to God', Cranmer, envious rather than waspish, responds 'You're very sure of that, Sir Thomas'. Not a question, either, but a witnessing to the obvious. The scene is unhistorical, and even most unlikely. We can only trust that More's 1 July 1535 prayer has been heard, and that these two Thomases are, like Stephen and Saul, 'both twain holy saints in heaven' (Roper, p.96; Harpsfield, p.197).

William Warham, too, we have already encountered, as Erasmus' patron, and through his place in the early stages of the Nun's affair. Stapleton published portions of the letter More wrote him in 1516, soon after Warham had resigned the Chancellorship of England. It begins thus: 'I have always reckoned you fortunate, when you discharged the function of Chancellor with distinction, and more fortunate now that you have freed yourself from it; you can enjoy a most welcome leisure that enables you to live for yourself and for God.' [27] Two years later, writing to Oxford University, he boldly vouches support for Greek studies from the university's chancellor, who in his Latin is *Reverendissimus in Christo Pater, Cantuariensis Antistes, qui et cleri totius nostri Primas est* (Rogers, p. 118). To counter a monk's attack on Erasmus, More invokes three prelates who patronize the Dutch scholar, and the formulation itself is interesting: *Coletum ... Reverendum Patrem Roffensem Episcopum ... Reverendissimum Cantuariensis Ecclesiae Pontificem* (Rogers, p. 169); very seldom in humanist Latin is *Pontifex* used of anyone but the Pope. More must have been pleased and proud to be able to explain to Erasmus that, if Warham had not left any bequest for him in his last will, it was because he died very poor, leaving barely £30 for the expenses of his funeral (Allen, ep. 2831).

John Morton, who became archbishop of Canterbury on 6 November 1486, when More was nearing his tenth birthday, is quoted as prophesying that the engaging lad Thomas, waiting on his guests at Lambeth Palace, would 'prove a marvellous man' (*Roper*, p.5). That 'wise and learned prelate ... placed him at Oxford' (p.5) and no doubt at Canterbury College, where most of the students were Benedictine monks belonging to Christ Church monastery, Canterbury.

Morton looms large in More's works. He had been dead fifteen years or so, and was remembered chiefly as an instrument of Henry VII's fiscal rigours, not to say exactions, when More, in *The History of King Richard III*, wrote this admiring and affectionate evocation beginning with Morton's imprisonment by Richard the usurper and his skilful manipulation of Buckingham into rebellion against the King

> For he, being as ye have heard, after King Edward's death, first taken by the tyrant for his truth to the king, found the mean to set this duke in his top, joined gentlemen together in aid of King Henry, devising first the marriage between him and King Edward's daughter, by which his faith declared and good service to both his masters at once, with infinite benefit to the realm by the conjunction of those two bloods in one, whose several titles had long unquieted the land; he fled the realm, went to Rome, never minding more to meddle with the world till the noble prince King Henry VII gat him home again,

made him archbishop of Canterbury and chancellor of England, whereunto the pope joined the honour of cardinal. Thus living many days in as much honour as one man might well wish, ended them so godly that his death with God's mercy well changed his life.[28] This man, therefore, as I was about to tell you, by the long and often alternate proof as well of prosperity as adverse fortune, had gotten by great experience, the very mother and mistress of wisdom, a deep insight in politic worldly drifts (*CW2*, p.91)

The tribute is generous. Not all historians would see Morton as a reluctant statesman, or give him the main credit for achieving the coalescence of the two Roses. Oxford University remembered her alumnus, Morton, with affection and petitioned for his release when he was in prison.

The acquaintance which enabled John More to secure for his son the privilege of living under the roof of Lambeth Palace may have matured into some friendship between Thomas and his former host; to Morton he seems to have owed much of the information about the last throes of the dynastic wars. A later relationship was formed when John Morton, the cardinal's grandnephew, married Helen Roper, a sister of William Roper, and thus became brother-in-law to More's eldest daughter Margaret.

The portrait of Morton in *Utopia* is better known, because it was published, and over the centuries it has reached almost every language. Its date is 1516, when More wrote Book I to put a firm dose of Western fact into his antipodean travelogue. Readers often wonder to what extent the Portuguese narrator Raphael resembles Thomas More. At least he uses the same style of clerical etiquette when he introduces Morton as *reuerendissimo patri Ioanni Mortono, Cantuariensi Archiepiscopo et Cardinali* (*CW4*, p.58). He stresses the 'reverence' of a prelate 'not more venerable through his authority [meaning his office] than by his prudence and virtue'. *Prudentia* is mentioned twice, and it would be tempting to render it by *wisdom* (to echo the English of *Richard III*) or to translate *prudentia rerum* by 'experience', again in imitation of More. At the end of the portrait drawn by Raphael, More, or rather the *persona* Morus, says: 'Listening to you, I felt as though I were becoming a child again through the pleasant recollection of that cardinal at whose court I was brought up as a child.'[29] Over one half of Raphael's *sermo* in Book I is devoted to his interview with Morton (in about 1497). He, the lone thinker, comes so near, in that scene, to playing the role of a counsellor to government that Morus seizes the opportunity to urge him toward public service.

More, among the qualities of Morton, has singled out *iuris magna peritia* (*CW*4, p.58): knowledge and practise of the law are common denominators among chancellors, and in that respect Wolsey was something of an exception. Becket himself was a fully trained lawyer; Archbishop Theobald saw to that by sending him to the best jurists of Christendom at Bologna, which then shone at its brightest with Gratian compiling the *Decretum*, while another professor would soon rule the Church as Alexander III.

I referred to Reginald Pole in evoking the day in November 1554 when Archdeacon Harpsfield welcomed him as he was crossing Canterbury on his way from Dover to London. Pole was coming to England as a legate *a latere*, that is, with full powers from the pope to decide, to excommunicate, to reconcile, etc. Becket and Wolsey had exercised such prerogatives with vigour. But Pole did not enter Canterbury as legate, nor use the title until Queen Mary expressly asked him to do so. Nor was he yet archbishop: he would be consecrated in March 1556, after the death of Cranmer.[30] But he enjoyed great prestige: he was a prince of the blood and a prince of the Church. Had he worked at it ever so little, he could have been elected pope after the death of Paul III, and he could have become King of England by marrying his cousin Mary Tudor. He was a confessor of the faith, in so far as his departure for Italy in 1531 was self-inflicted exile, after he had rebuked Henry VIII over the divorce, and refused to succeed Wolsey as archbishop of York. This was at a time when Warham was still primate, and when More was chancellor: while they chose to wait and see, Pole voiced his opposition in a stormy interview with the king. No wonder that Harpsfield praised him, in 1566, as a man who, 'besides his noble birth, is such that England perhaps never produced anyone better or more learned, and whose reputation for singular holiness and erudition has filled Europe.'[31]

In his famous *Pro ecclesiasticae unitatis defensione* written largely under the impact of the execution of Fisher and More, Pole refers neither to Cranmer, nor to any archbishop of Canterbury, except St Augustine, to remind Henry VIII that 'Gregory, a successor of Peter' had taken the initiative of evangelizing England.[32] Little did he expect that he would occupy the primatial see and that his mortal remains would be laid to rest in the Chapel of St Thomas the Martyr in Christ Church Cathedral. Since it is Thomas More that brings us together, I shall quote a few lines from Pole's address to the City of London in which he compares More to Socrates, as countless biographers and commentators were to do in his wake. In a tragedy played at Athens, the sentence 'You have killed the best man of all the Greeks' inflamed the spectators with anger at the murderers of Socrates:

> By how much more just anger and compassion should you, the city of London, be stirred? You did not hear these words uttered by chance once in a theatre in your own country by some actor, but you were compelled to hear this charge 'You have killed, you have killed the best of all Englishmen!' brought against you by the most serious men at a time when they were speaking most seriously in every place now Christian in name.[33]

Pole also writes that he is proud of having been a friend of Fisher and More, a bond he prizes above his familiarity with all the princes and kings now living.[34] Born in 1500, when More was 23, he was schooled at the Sheen Charterhouse, where John Colet too resorted and would die in 1519, and which More would haunt during his years of retirement. Pole returned to Sheen from time to time in periods of crisis to bask in the devotion of the monks and steel himself for resistance and also to study theology. Before receiving the most refined education at Paris and Padua, he took his B.A. at Oxford. His tutors were More's friends William Latimer and Thomas Linacre. His guest at Padua was Thomas Lupset, to whom in 1517 Guillaume Budé had dedicated his preface to the Paris edition of More's Utopia. Stapleton has preserved a letter More wrote, circa 1518, jointly to Pole and John Clement, his former protégé, and eventually the husband of his adopted daughter Margaret Gygs. More acknowledges receipt of a prescription made by Clement and of the corresponding medicine, prepared by Pole's mother, the Countess of Salisbury, *feminarum optima atque nobilissima*, (Rogers, ep.71, p.136). In 1535, Pole procured an Italian edition of the report on the trial and death of More, and he expanded on it in his own *De Unitate* (as the 1536 book is usually short-titled). He served England more as legate than as primate, since by 1551 he was a sick man as well as totally out of favour with the irascible Pope Paul IV, who held him to be a heretic and summoned him to his Roman tribunal. Queen Mary intercepted these papal dispatches and died peacefully at Whitehall twelve hours before her cousin the cardinal died across the Thames in Lambeth Palace.

Pole was a confessor of the faith through his exile, and the proud son of a martyr through the execution of his mother Margaret, who had been governess of Princess Mary Tudor. The bishops he selected, without any interference from the Crown, were a different breed from the lawyers and diplomats promoted by the early Tudor monarchs. As scholars and men of God, they had their prototype in St Anselm of Canterbury, who had been Anselm of Bec, and before that, Anselm of Aosta. English by his episcopal appointment reluctantly accepted, Anselm belonged to a line of primates who, with roots both continental and monastic, were disposed and fitted to protest against the excessive nationalization of the *Ecclesia anglicana* which to them meant provincial isolation. Becket, though born in London, adopted the style and the stand of those predecessors: his master Theobald had been Anselm's successor twice, at the Norman Abbey, then at Christ Church, as Anselm had twice succeeded Lanfranc.

It was to Anselm that Becket looked up. Even his devotion to St Elphege was a debt to Anselm, as we have seen (footnote 17). Taking a less canonical view of martyrdom than Lanfranc, Anselm prepared Becket to conclude unhesitatingly that, if one witnessed to the freedom of the

Church, one witnessed to the rights and honour of God. Anselm was 'a man utterly given up to God, deeply and quietly intent on the contemplation of truths of faith which gave him spiritual, moral, intellectual and aesthetic pleasure all at once'.[35] He alone, of all *Cantuarienses*, as also of Europe's huge army of black monks, shines as a star of the first magnitude in the galaxy of Christian thinkers and mystics. His *Fides quaerens intellectum* has become the maxim of theological reflection; his *Cur Deus homo*, written in the monastic leisure of exile, has become the most illustrious expression and specimen of that faith-inspired ambition to understand God's order.

More is credited with possessing a volume of Anselm's works and letters in a manuscript on parchment now preserved at the British Museum.[36] He does not quote him often, chiefly, no doubt, because his friend Erasmus gave priority to the critical edition of the early Fathers over the medieval luminaries; yet two of these, Bernard and Anselm, are More's best allies in demonstrating to his daughter, and through her to many thousands of readers, that ecclesial consensus, which for him is the main seat of infallibility, is a gradual achievement. Bernard, he says, 'that holy devout man' and a lover of Our Lady if ever there was one, disapproved of the feast of her Conception, as did other 'right holy men too. Now was there on the other side the blessed holy bishop St Anselm'. Despite this disagreement 'they be both twain holy saints in heaven' (Rogers, pp.525-526). Notice that More calls him 'Saint' Anselm, again following a consensus of God's people before the Roman magisterium had endorsed it explicitly.

Anselm chafed against the political entanglement from the beginning of his primatial career. The see had been vacant for four years by the ill-will of King William Rufus. To accept it, Anselm needed permission from his own feudal lord, Robert, Duke of Normandy, a brother, though no friend, of England's king. And hardly had he arrived when Rufus wanted church money in order to conquer Normandy. Anselm refused, and in protest fled the realm to seek the pope's arbitration. He returned at the accession of Henry I, but, as the new king demanded too binding an allegiance, he preferred a second exile to compromise. It needed the pope to temper this intransigence, and come to terms with royal greed, as sixty years later Alexander III would advocate yielding to some claims of Henry II, and another sixty years later, Innocent III would blame Langton for overly humiliating John Lackland. A pattern of almost arrogant provocative opposition seemed to characterize Canterbury. Anselm had initiated it; Becket's martyrdom had sealed it. Langton's seal bore this inscription: *Mors expressa foris tibi vita sit intus amoris*, addressed to his slain predecessor: 'May this representation of death mean a life of love within you'.

Warham, though a canon lawyer and a careerist, was haunted by Becket's image when the hour of conflict came. What to those prelates was freedom from secular control became for Cranmer freedom from foreign control, at a period when the papacy could be viewed as no longer a centre of unity but an obstacle to much needed renovation. A time, also, when the prestige of the Old Testament, rediscovered through Hebrew philology, produced such models as Joshua and David, who had ruled the Jewish clergy along with the nation.

MORE AN OFFICIAL GUEST OF CANTERBURY

As well as the end of various pilgrims' ways, Canterbury was a major stage on the road between London and the Channel. Thomas More may have stayed the night there on several of his trips to the Continent, especially during his official missions, when etiquette demanded that he travel at a slow pace to and from Boulogne or Calais. He was in the numerous party which crowded Canterbury in the Spring of 1520, the year of the third centennial of Becket's translation, a jubilee year. Being still but a junior minister, he was only 'Mr More, a squire of Middlesex', but in the list we see him first named of esquires.[37] He was in the retinue of the king, who was on his way to the spectacular encounter with Francis I of France at the 'Field of Cloth of Gold'. A manuscript account at the Bodleian Library shows the royal company reaching Canterbury on Thursday 24th May, and tarrying until Tuesday 29th May, the last stage having been from Charing, no doubt because the Archbishop had a manor there. The season was not that of the pardon (7 July), but that of Becket's ordination (Pentecost week). The point of tarrying in the religious capital of the realm was that Charles V and his queen were expected to arrive there as pilgrims, a summit meeting under the aegis of the martyr who had taught Christian princes the limits of their power. The emperor was only twenty, nine years younger than Henry VIII and had been elected less than a year before. He was welcomed at Dover by Cardinal Wolsey, and lodged for the night at the famous castle. The king waited until after midnight of the Saturday before riding by torchlight to meet his guest.

> On the morrow, which was Whitsunday, the king and the emperor with all the other estate rode unto Canterbury... till they came to Christ Church, whereas they were received with general procession by the Lord of Canterbury [Warham] and two other mitred. The emperor and the king went both under the canopy unto St Thomas' shrine, whereas they made their prayers and oblations unto that blessed saint.[38]

It was at the archbishops palace that Catherine of Aragon, now aged 38, first saw her sister Juana's son, king of Spain and emperor. Then all went together to the High Mass on that solemn day of Pentecost. On Whit Monday they banqueted, and on Tuesday 'these estates departed out of Canterbury'.

While Wolsey was welcoming the emperor at Dover, on Pentecost Eve, More wrote a long letter to Erasmus, a councillor of Charles, the triple topic being other subjects of his imperial majesty: two scholars recommended by Erasmus, and the promising Spanish humanist Juan Luis Vives — it looks as if the enforced leisure of this waiting period had given him the chance of reading Vives in great doses. One paragraph of his letter is news: 'The emperor is landing in England today. The king will meet him tomorrow, or perhaps during the night, which is now beginning to fall. The king, and the nobles and all the people rejoice at the message confirming that the landing has taken place'.[39]

It seems that More was on close attendance upon Henry VIII. Writing may not have been easy with so many courtiers around, most of them above his rank. He may have sought refuge in the library of Christ Church monastery. William Selling, the protohumanist prior, had provided glass windows to make it a better place for students. Selling, born in the village of that name, near Canterbury, had been Henry VII's main envoy in 1487 for the inauguration of Innocent VIII, and had given a speech which impressed the Roman Curia by its Latin elegance.[40] Selling took with him his Canterbury-born godson Thomas Linacre, who remained behind and spent many years in Italy. Now Linacre was More's tutor in the Greek language, and later his house-guest and close friend. He may have been a significant link with the metropolitan chapter.[41] Thomas Goldwell, who had been prior since 1517, may have been another link having studied at Canterbury College, Oxford. He must have been over-monastic in Cranmer's opinion, since he was not made dean of the secular chapter which was instituted at the dissolution of the monastery, but pensioned off. More may also have visited Greyfriars, since the Franciscan Order appealed to him most, and we have seen him accommodating the Canterbury guardian under his roof. In the matter of the Nun, in fact, no Benedictine monk approached More, hence his protestation to Cromwell that the government should suspect no disloyalty 'in my communication either with the nun or the friars'. (*Rogers* p.492)

In 1527, More was again a sojourner at Canterbury in an official capacity, as part of the mission Wolsey was fulfilling as royal plenipotentiary. Meanwhile he had become a senior minister, a knight, and chancellor of the Duchy of Lancaster. The situation, too, had drastically changed in Europe and in Christendom. In 1520, both Henry and Charles were able to pay homage to Becket's shrine without any embarrassment. They vied with each other in being good sons of the Church. The indulgence of the jubilee, which they were entitled to receive, was seen as a blessing from the Holy Father as well as a share in the martyr's merits. Many crowned heads had bowed to this tomb. Louis VII of France crossed the Channel only for that purpose. Richard Coeur de Lion visited his island kingdom only once, and his purpose was to seek the holy blissful martyr for whose death his own father carried the main responsibility. But Wolsey's 1527 expedition was prompted by his royal master's plan to get his first marriage annulled, and the juncture looked the more favourable as Clement VII was a prisoner in his own Castel S. Angelo, and could not be reached. Wolsey, as senior legate-for-life, dreamt of a council at Avignon which he would control, and which would meet Henry's desire. As *defensor fidei,* the king of England claimed to be a more Catholic prince than Charles V, who had allowed, almost encouraged, Lutheran mercenaries to sack the Eternal City in May 1527.

The few days of Wolsey at Canterbury culminated on Sunday 7 July, the very feast-day of the Translation, when he presided at the solemn liturgy. The special intention of the public prayer was the deliverance of the pope. We have, this time, no echo from More's pen. Erasmus' boy-and-postman was in the party and at Calais More would let him go his way toward the Low Countries with some mail for his Flemish friends; most of these were angry with him for being in the retinue of the *Idole britannique*, as they called the proud cardinal, responsible in their eyes for the cold war between their countries.

WHO IS 'ST THOMAS OF LONDON'?

The son of Gilbert Becket was named Thomas because he was born on the feast of St Thomas the Apostle, Tuesday 21 December. The eldest son of John More was named Thomas because both his grandfathers were thus named, and so would his first grandson, and many others. In England christenings meant almost an alternation of John and Thomas, the latter name on account of the popular martyr, England's highest trophy in the spiritual realm. The very fact that there are two of them, fellows as Londoners, and as chancellors, and as kings' best friends and most famous victims, prompts people like me to call them Becket and More, even to index them in *Moreana* under those surnames. London possessed a hospital and chapel endowed by Becket's sister, and officially named St Thomas of Acon, from a crusading connection with that city in Palestine, but the populace called it 'Becket's House'.[42] This label made the saint a neighbour, another citizen of London.

The reference to St Thomas' Eve in More's last letter may raise the question: how comes he does not mention Becket at all until that eve of his own death? I can suggest a few reasons:

1. When More fights for the Church, even while he is still in public office, a wind of animosity blows against Becket. We learn from More's *Debellation* that 'some heretics ... pulled down of late upon London Bridge the image of the blessed martyr St Thomas' (*CW*10 p.16). It is enough to protest against this assault. It might be unwise to trumpet the martyr's name in and out of season.[43]

2. One step further is to canonize rival St Thomases. The name was so popular that it abounds in More's own account of the heretics brought to his tribunal: Bilney, Benet, Harding, Hitton. In the primer published by George Joye, *Ortulus animae*, to wean the faithful from the Catholic Book of Hours, St Polycarp's name on 23 February is replaced by that of 'St Thomas the Martyr', that is, Hitton, burnt at the stake on that date, at Maidstone. More rejects the new saint as 'the devil's stinking martyr'. (*CW*8, p.17 and cf n. to *CW*9, p.93).

3. More will not sound the praises of national patrons. He never names St George, to my knowledge. He takes a monk to task for yielding to the common tendency to make more of what is our own than of what is universal, though he does not 'criticize any nation for fostering the cult of some saint when it has a good reason to do so' (*CW*15, p.279), *nominatim* says the Latin (p.278) and he himself hardly drops a name when speaking of martyrs in the *Dialogue of Comfort*, except those of the Bible.[44]

4. Like Anselm before him, Becket fought as a hierarch invested with specific rights for him to steward and defend. They opposed specific practices which are detrimental to the autonomy of the realm spiritual, especially the creation of bishops and abbots by the secular sovereign. More's ground is broader and touches the very constitution of the Church. Becket's terrain lends itself to compromise and concordat, and saints like Fisher and More had come to terms with a *modus vivendi* which allowed Henry VII to choose his bishops more freely than Anselm and Becket would have

accepted. More's cause does not belong to canon law at all, but to the Catholic faith. Harpsfield, as we saw, harps on that string; he evoked St Thomas of Dover rather than Elphege because he wanted Thomases compared, but that monk, like Elphege, died to protect the treasure of the community (pp. 214-215). Of More he writes: 'This man is therefore our blessed protomartyr of all the laity for the preservation of the unity of Christ's Church' (p. 213).

5. The style is the man, and here we can contrast the styles. Becket's had an element of defiance, if not provocation, while lying low and keeping quiet was essential to More's spirit and to his strategy. Pole goes to great lengths to insist that silence befitted More, and did not make him a lesser martyr than the outspoken Fisher.

6. We possess some two hundred letters of Becket, some of which explain and justify his position and attitude. Not all of these were available to More. At the point of death, no reservation remained in his cult for a saint whose death had become a paradigm, as it were, of modern martyrdom, especially where a disciple of Christ is persecuted by fellow-Christians. Is it not impressive that the place of Becket's murder should be called *martyrium, martyrdom*? And befitting that his ancient shrine should now include a chapel honouring the saints and martyrs of our time, 'to demonstrate', as a former dean puts it, 'that Christianity is as demanding and costly today as it has ever been'?.[45]

No wonder our Thomases have been contrasted more often than compared. Robert Speaight, who played the part of the archbishop in many early productions of Eliot's play, in far--flung countries as well as England, published *Thomas Becket* in 1938 (London: Longmans) and has this to say in the Introduction: St Thomas 'does not come down to us with quite the charm, humility and lucid strength of St Thomas More... But the hero is not always endowed with perfect intellectual discretion — and neither is the saint' (p.x).

One area of contrast is the tempo of their respective canonisations: Becket made it within the third year of his death, More not till the 400th year. Some people have imagined wild reasons for these four centuries of waiting, reckoning for instance that some *advocatus diaboli* produced unedifying pages from *Utopia*. A defrocked French Benedictine, Nicolas de Gueudeville, in a *Vie de Thomas Morus* prefixed to his 1715 translation of *Utopia*, says: 'I am amazed that More has not yet been placed in the Martyrology ... If there exists any jealousy among the saints, he should envy the good fortune of Becket... If anything, More is the more canonisable of the two. Becket was the victim of a surprise assassination. Had he been in More's place, would he have met the challenge as perfectly? His courage, nay his obstinacy, were exercised in defending ecclesiastical law, whereas More offered his neck, gave his head, for the supremacy of the Tiara.'[46] I have compressed a little this rather ill-informed facile parallel. Gueudeville thinks that canonisation is the pope's initiative; it is not, but rather a *vox populi* endorsed by the supreme pontiff. That call from below, from the grass-roots, was immediate in the case of Becket, as of Francis of Assisi. Not of More: even Roper never uses the word 'martyr' of his father-in-law. More waited two weeks less than John Fisher, thirty-five years less than the Carthusian martyrs he saw going to their death on 4 May 1535 and who were not canonised till 1970. What about Joan of Arc, who died (also at the hands of fellow-Catholics) in 1431 and was canonised in 1920?

The medieval knight, a lover of the horse and the hunt, who embraced the monastic mould, and the Renaissance humanist who ran his household *more monastico*, have become inseparable. The same Anglican parson, W.H. Hutton, published a *Becket* in 1889 and a *More* in 1894. The same agnostic French playwright Jean Anouilh published a *Becket* in 1959 and a *More* in 1987. The two saints have escaped the hands of historians to become
mythical figures: R.W. Chambers examined *The Saga and the Myth of Thomas More* in an Oxford University Press booklet of 1926, and Jean-Marie Grassin devoted a voluminous Sorbonne dissertation in 1975 to *Le Mythe de Thomas Becket au théâtre*. As John of Salisbury says in reference to the legends about Becket's mother — whether Saxon or Saracen: 'Brave legends both! They mean Becket's great'.[47] The two Thomases were great at each stage of their variegated existence, and both greatest in the last act of their

play. That the translation of one coincides with the decapitation of the other makes it tempting, and I hope not unfruitful, to admire and emulate both in what they share, that which is the essence of all martyrdom — 'to obey God rather than man' (Acts 5, 29).

NOTES

Throughout this book the initials '*CW*' with volume and page number indicate the critical edition *The Complete Works of St Thomas More*, ed. Daniel Kinney (Yale University Press, 1986).

1 *The Correspondence of Sir Thomas More,* ed. Elizabeth Frances Rogers. Princeton University Press, 1947, p.564, lines 18-22.
2 Henry II died in France on 6 July 1189. John Hus was burnt at the stake in Constance on 6 July 1415. Richard III and Queen Anne were crowned in Westminster Abbey on 6 July 1483. More himself, in Wolsey's retinue, celebrated the vigil of St Thomas in Christ Church, Canterbury, on 6 July 1527. He may not have been aware of the other coincidences.
3 *The Life of Sir Thomas More, Knight*, by William Roper, ed. Elsie Vaughan Hitchcock, Early English Text Society (London, 1935), p.96, lines 8-10. More's 'consented' reflects the Latin Vulgate at Acts 8:1 (erat *consentiens* neci eius) and Acts 22:20 (ego astabam et *consentiebam*). Further references to Roper's biography will be given in parenthesis within the text, with numbers of page and lines.
   More's growing relationship with Simon Peter during his fifteen months in the Tower — which was under the patronage of St Peter-in-Chains — is documented in my seven page essay, 'Saint Pierre', *Thomas More et la bible* (Paris: Vrin, 1969), 429-434. In *Richard III*, More echoes the tradition that the Abbey was consecrated by St Peter 'in person' on the Sunday when Bishop Mellitus was to have held the ceremony (*CW*2, p.28)
4 Dominic Baker-Smith, *More's Utopia*, Harper Collins Academic, 1991, p.12.
5 'quo (nisi me fallit opinio) nullus ordo sanctior', is a cautious phrasing; 'no order is holier' does not place the Friars Minor above similar apostolic orders. More is writing this to a complacent Carthusian — see *Humanist Letters*, *CW*15. p.294, and Rogers, ep.201.
6 'St Thomas More as Church Patron', by Seymour House, *Journal of Ecclesiastical History*, 40,2 (April 1989), p.209.
7 Claude Jenkins, *Sir Thomas More: A Commemoration Lecture*, (Canterbury Papers, 5) Canterbury, 1935.
8 Münster: Aschendorf, 1966, pp.90-91. The title means 'new letters', i.e., added to the edition by Rogers. The 35 lines are rather

impersonal, and one imagines other benefactors receiving the same generous compliments. The blank left for Alice's name shows how unimportant socially the chancellor's wife was. No chancellor in centuries had been a married man, and not a few, including More's host, John Morton, had been, *qua* Archbishops of Canterbury, Abbots of Christ Church Abbey.

9 *CW*7, p.415, where Simon Fish's text is reproduced as an appendix to More's retort. Because of the huge influence the pamphlet had exerted right from the day Anne Boleyn put it in Henry VIII's hands, it has been reprinted scores of times as an Anglican classic, and incorporated in full into Foxe's *Book of Martyrs*.

10 Roper, p.93, where More tells his judges that the act of parliament on which his indictment is grounded 'was contrary to the laws and statutes of our own land yet unrepealed, as they might evidently perceive in 'Magna Charta': *Quod eccelesia anglicana libera sit, et habeat omnia iura sua integra et libertates suas illaesas.*'

11 *The Colloquies of Erasmus,* translated by Craig R. Thompson (The University of Chicago Press, 1965) pp.310-311. The original Latin is in *Erasmi Opera Omnia*, I-3, *Colloquia*, ed. Léon-E.Halkin (Amsterdam, 1972) from p.486/589ff. Erasmus mentions both monasteries, uses 'majestic' three times to define the cathedral, describes the stone statues of the three [sic] murderers. He willingly kissed the rusty sword *amore martyris* (lines 626-9), and a cloth stained by Becket's blood. He accepts that liturgical vessels may be precious, but is unhappy about accumulated treasures which are never put to use; they are only shown behind locks and padlocks, whereas Becket, were he here, would bestow their value on feeding and clothing the poor, who are living temples of God. (The siglum for the Amsterdam edition is ASD.)

12 Charles Duggan, 'The Significance of the Becket Dispute in the History of the English Church', *Ampleforth Journal*, Autumn 1970, p.375. This is quoted in other accounts of the year 1532.

13 'La sainteté de Thomas Becket à travers les verrières de Sens et de Chartres du début du XIIIe siècle', by Colette et Jean-Paul Deremble, *Saints et Sainteté hier et aujourd'hui*, ed. Christiane d'Haussy (Paris, 1991), pp.39-59.

14 *Opera Omnia*, ASD I-3, pp.257/792-94. C.R.Thompson's translation in *Colloquies*, p.70.

15 See my *The Bible in the Works of Thomas More*, Part III (Nieuwkoop: De Graaf, 1970), p.148 under Hebrews 13:14. More like Wyclif uses 'dwelling' as the epithet, to render the Vulgate *manentem*. Hebrews 11: 13-14 is echoed in More's 'Dialogue of Comfort': 'In what country soever we walk in this world, we be but as pilgrims and wayfaring men' (*CW*12, p.251/19). This is our chance of also quoting Chaucer's *Canterbury Tales*. Old Egeus, a pagan, says in the 'Knight's Tale' (lines 2796-97):

This world nys but a thurghfare ful of wo,
And we be pilgrymes, passynge to and fro.

16 From *Murder in the Cathedral* (1935), first staged in Canterbury.
17 Eliot's spelling 'Elphege' tallies with John of Salisbury's Latin 'Elphegus'in the *Vita Anselmi*, written at Becket's request to further Anselm's canonisation. Lanfranc had some misgivings about the local cult, because Elphege, killed by the Danes in 1020, had not died 'for the faith'. When Anselm, who had succeeded Lanfranc as Prior of Bec, visited England in 1033-34, his opinion was sought, and he answered unhesitatingly: 'Since Elphege died for justice, he witnessed for Christ, who is justice.' Lanfranc then instituted a solemn yearly feast. *Vita di Anselmo d'Aosta*, a bilingual edition 'a cura de Inos Biffi' (Milano: Jaca, 1989), p.60.
18 The apostrophe did not exist in More's day. My adding it is part of the normalization of spelling. Jean Plaidy goes one step further with her historical novel *St Thomas's Eve* (1954, Pan Books 1966, seventh printing 1977).
19 On More's rapport with the aboriginal Thomas, see my *A Name for All Seasons, - Essential Articles for the Study of Thomas More* (Hamden, CT: Archon, 1977), pp.558-61. The harsh remarks occur in volumes of controversy where More analyses the act of faith and the role of human witnesses in eliciting it (*CW7*, pp.195 and 197; *CW8*, pp.542, 547, 553, 615, 747-748, 975). That More never quotes the moving words 'My Lord and my God!' does not indicate that he never repeated them.
  Stonyhurst College in Lancashire possesses a gold cross donated to its Continental ancestor on 29 June 1755 by Father Thomas More, S.J., as a relic of Thomas More. Inside the cross is a relic of Thomas the Apostle identified by this Greek caption: *Tou apostolou Thomas leipsanon tode.* See *Life of Blessed Thomas More*, by Thomas Bridgett, London: Burns & Oates, 2nd ed. (1892), p.456.
20 '*Esset*, inquit, *ille dies mihi conueniens. Et quare? Quia dies ille Translatio erat sancti Thomae Cantuariensis, etsi non publice festus, tamen in Ecclesia magnopere celebratus ... Non igitur immerito in translatione gloriosa Sancti Thomae martyris, patroni sui, transferri quoque ex his tenebris ad lucem, et martyr fieri Thomas Morus voluit.*' (Ch.19, p.68 in the 1689 edition of Gratz). My rendering keeps to Stapleton's Latin more closely than does Hallett in his translation *The Life of Sir Thomas More* (London, Burns & Oates 1928) p.204-5.
21 More uses 'wretched' a lot, but 'wicked' only to designate malice proceeding from the devil. He was predisposed in the nun's favour by four bodies of religious men, the Benedictines, the Franciscans, the Bridgettines, the Carthusians, and he must have been dismayed by the failure of these professionals to discern the 'undeceivable tokens'

68

which (he will say) betray the presence of the evil spirit (*CW*12, p.133/4, in a passage which also recommends Jean Gerson's *De probatione spirituum*). But then Gerson himself was deceived when he distrusted the visions of St Bridget of Sweden, duly acknowledged afterwards through her canonisation. More, in this context, quotes 2 Cor 11:14 and 1 John 4:1.

22 The inflation of oaths under Henry VIII had so devalued their sacrosanctity that Cranmer himself stated, on 30 March 1533, that his oath of allegiance to the pope, a necessary step toward receiving the pallium, was made *pro forma potius quam pro esse*. No wonder he was, not only annoyed, but baffled, by More's fastidious refusal to swear to a text without making sure that he endorsed every word in it.

23 In *Thomas More* (London: Jonathan Cape, 1935) p.303. Other commentators wonder if More was not being ironical.

24 Cardinal Thomas Bourchier is in centre stage through all the pages in *Richard III* which deal with the right of sanctuary, mostly in dialogue with the queen herself, reluctant to let go of her little prince. The Protector calls him *reuerendissimus iste pater ... cardinalis*, in English: 'our reverend Father here present, my lord Cardinal' (*CW*2 p.26). That is expected in direct style. But afterwards, he is 'the Lord Cardinal', or, about as often as not, plain 'the cardinal', in Latin always plain *cardinalis*. At one point More calls him 'Archbishop of York' (pp.27 and 28), obviously from the fact that his predecessor as chancellor, Thomas Rotherham, was my Lord of York. Bourchier's 32-year pontificate ended on 6 April 1486, and included his coronation of Henry VII.

25 See Rogers p.495, and above all *The Divorce Tracts of Henry VIII*, ed. by Edward Surtz, S.J. and Virginia Murphy (Angers: *Moreana* 1988). This book includes the full text of the answers from the foreign universities which approved of the king's 'divorce', with the much longer defence and illustration of those answers by Henry VIII's own canonists, Cranmer being the master-mind of the 1531 publication, as he had been the conceiver of the whole consultation plan.

26 He is credited with pleading with Henry VIII in favour of at least one queen, and of Thomas Cromwell.

27 This is the beautiful Latin original: *Semper quidem felicem paternitatis tuae sortem iudicaui, et dum Cancellariae munere prae-clare fungereris, et nunc feliciorem, postquam eodem defunctus in otium optatissimum, quo tibi possis ac Deo viuere, secessisti* (Rogers, p.86).

28 The sentence 'his death well changed his life' is not crystal clear. In my opinion, it echoes the *vita mutatur non tollitur* of the preface of the mass for the dead. Death is a mere change in a man's life, and a pious death is a change for the better, a winning exchange, a 'gain' as St Paul says (Phil 1:21). Thus More canonises Morton, who, as early as 1483, is made to say he means to spend his life with his breviary

and his rosary, to 'meddle with his book and his beads and no further' (*CW*2, p.92)

29 I have repeated 'child' in fidelity to More's repeating of 'puer': *uisus mihi interim sum ... repuerascere quodammodo iucunda recordatione Cardinalis illius, in cuius aula puer sum educatus* (*CW*4, p.86/1-3). Morton's palace is the theatre of more than half of Raphael's 'sermo' in Book I of *Utopia*: the Portuguese sailor begins to speak in his own voice at p.54, reaches Morton's presence at p.58 and stays there until p.84 of a book ending on p.108.

30 Pole was ordained a priest on 20 March 1556, celebrated his first Mass on the 21st, the very day of Cranmer's martyrdom, and was consecrated bishop on the 22nd.

31 Harpsfield calls Pole '*virum certe talem, ut praeter generis nobilitatem, nesciam an meliorem eo et doctiorem Anglia unquam pepererit, qui singularis sanctitatis et eruditionis suae fama Europam implevit*'. *Dialogi Sex* by Alan Cope, a pseudonym for Harpsfield, first published 1566, quoted here from the 1573 edition (Antwerp: Plantin) p.551.

32 *Pole's Defence of the Unity of the Church*, translated with introduction by Joseph G. Dwyer, Westminster Maryland; Newman Press (1965) p.106.

33 Dwyer, p.232. This purple passage is quoted by Stapleton in the final chapter of his *Vita Mori*, and this is how Hallett transposes the key-sentence: 'Ye have put to death him who was the noblest of all the English' (p.219). The Latin (from *Liber Tertius*):'*quanto nunc iustiore et odio et misericordia commoueri debes, ciuitas Londinensis, quae eadem illa uerba, non domi in theatro tuo semel ab aliquo histrione, casu prolata, sed omnibus iam christiani nominis locis, a grauissimis uiris, tum cum maxime serio loquuntur, tibi saepius exprobata, excipere cogeris, Interfecistis, interfecistis hominem omnium Anglorum optimum*' (Ed. princeps, fol. XCIV-XCV). The passage with generous context will be found in *Moreana* no. 3 (June 1964), 'Thomas More, le meilleur des Anglais' (pp.23-35) in the translation of Noelle-Marie Egretier.

34 The Latin is given in *Neue Briefe*, p.88. In Pole's 'encomium Mori', *prudentia summa* is used twice to stress in More the quality he himself stressed in Morton. He is also called *pater patriae*. Margaret Roper's passionate kisses and embraces of 1 July 1535 are narrated in detail.

35 G.R. Evans as quoted by Jeffrey Dodds in 'St Anselm's Understanding of the Atonement', *Ushaw Magazine* (1991-2) p.44 — a dissertation for the University of Durham Certificate in Theology.

36 The reference, *MS. Royal 5 F.IX*, is provided in *Neue Briefe*, p.85.

37 Joycelyne Gledhill Russell, *The Field of Cloth of Gold* London: Routledge, 1969, p.198.

38 Reproduced in J.G. Russell's book as Appendix C from MS Ashmole 1116.

39 P.S. Allen, ed., *Opus epistolarum Des. Erasmi*, Oxford University Press, 1906-52, ep.1106. The text with English and French translations is reproduced in *Moreana* 113.

40 See David Knowles, OSB, *The Religious Orders in England*, vol. III, *The Tudor Age*, Cambridge University Press, 1959. Knowles devotes four pages to William Selling as an outstanding prior, and says that his D.D. at Bologna was a rare attainment for a black monk. At the Dissolution, six of the twelve prebendaries of the cathedral chapter were chosen out of the 79 monks who had constituted the priory.

41 Linacre was grammarian, physician to the king, and eventually also priest. He resided in St Benet's parish, London. More was one of his executors (1524). See my 'Thomas More and Thomas Linacre', *Moreana* 13/63-7 and my review of *Linacre Studies* in *Moreana* 61/53f. There is a Linacre Centre at Oxford and a *Linacre Quarterly*.

42 Acon is what we now call Acre, a seaport in North-West Israel which was captured by the Crusaders in 1191.

43 Tyndale already vilifies Becket as a traitor. The statue of Becket was restored under Queen Mary, and again mutilated in 1555, so much had the archbishop become a symbol of the old religion. The chapel to him in St Thomas'Tower was rededicated to the Apostle Thomas.

44 He does name a Romanus on p.246 of *A Dialogue of Comfort*, but prefers to evoke 'so many a thousand holy martyrs'(ib. *CW*12 p.316), as the *Te Deum* evokes the 'white-robed host of martyrs', and Hebrews 12:1 'a cloud of witnesses'

45 In 'Worldly Holiness', by Dean Victor de Waal, *Saints et sainteté hier et aujourd'hui*, ed. by Christiane d'Haussy (Paris:1991) p.206.

46 In the Introduction to this Amsterdam book the pages are not numbered; instead the printer has put asterisks at the bottom and the page from which we quote boasts five stars.

47 In the play *Saint Thomas of Canterbury* by Aubrey de Vere (1876), Act I, Sc 1.

VII The Right Honourable The Lord Rawlinson of Ewell P.C.,Q.C.

Born in 1919 and educated at Downside and Christ's College, Cambridge (Exhibitioner 1938; Hon. Fellow 1980), Peter Rawlinson was called to the Bar by the Inner Temple in 1946. He was appointed Q.C. in 1959; P.C. in 1964; Attorney General 1970-74; Attorney General for Northern Ireland 1972-74; Solicitor General 1962-64; Recorder of Kingston upon Thames 1975-85; M.P. for Epsom and Ewell 1974-78. He received a Knighthood in 1962 and retired from practice at the Bar in 1986. Publications include Public Duty and Personal Faith — the example of Thomas More.

When the Duke of Norfolk, Lord Treasurer of England, visited Chelsea Parish Church he saw his colleague the Lord High Chancellor of England singing at Mass in the parish choir. 'God's body', he exclaimed, 'God's body, my Lord Chancellor... A parish clerk! A parish clerk!'

The words express, probably, the genuine bewilderment, as well as reproach, felt by a pragmatical down-to-earth self-seeking fellow Minister at the humility and simplicity of the greatest man ever to bear the Great Seal of England.

Some four years later the same nobleman, sitting upon the Commission to try his former colleague in Westminster Hall (and probably equally bewildered by Thomas More's refusal to obey the King's demand to accept the King's new title of Supreme Head, and at his defence) commented: 'We now plainly see that ye are maliciously bent'.

What is plain to us to see is that Norfolk did not 'see' and did not understand, as he had never understood, the man who was once his colleague. To the very end the colleagues, even friends, of Thomas More still failed to understand that for Thomas More there existed a loyalty superior to that which he and they owed to Caesar.

One week ago this morning, I passed that Church where the Lord Chancellor sang as that 'parish clerk', which so offended the Duke. One week ago this evening, I passed on my way from the Debating Chamber in the House of Commons through the great Hall at Westminster (built some eight hundred years ago) and I stopped at the plaque which marks where Thomas More stood over 440 years ago when he faced his judges, and doubtless smiled sadly at Norfolk's comments.

Above my head was the great roof with its hammer beams, timber hewn from the New Forest where William Rufus died from the mysterious assassin's arrow. Before me, rose the great west window on either side, the stone walls rising to the wooden roof. Because it was night, and empty, and silent, and only partly lit, around me I could feel the spirits of many remarkable Englishmen, including a King, who had passed through that place to their deaths. For at night that Hall is a sinister place.

But my thoughts were only for that day of July 1st 1535, when the two Courts of Chancery and King's Bench were flung into one and a Lord Chancellor was tried, a precedent for the trial of that King one hundred years later. I thought of how the one Court formed on that day perhaps covered the spot where the prisoner, Thomas More, in happier times as Lord Chancellor on his way to his Court of Chancery knelt to receive the blessing of his father, a judge of the King's Bench.

Above all I seemed to hear what passed that day in that Court 400 years ago, and seemed to hear the voice of Richard Rich and the cross-examination by the prisoner — a cross-examination so deadly to the honour of that most vile of Solicitors General. I seemed to hear those great words spoken by More in rebuttal of the indictment:

> For as much, my Lord, this indictment is grounded upon an Act of Parliament directly repugnant to the laws of God and His Holy Church, the supreme government of which, or any part thereof, may no temporal prince presume by any law to take upon him, as rightly belonging to the See of Rome, a spiritual pre-eminence by the mouth of Our Saviour himself, *personally* present upon the earth, only to Saint Peter and his Successors, bishops of the same See by special prerogative granted. It is therefore in law amongst Christian men insufficient to charge any Christian Man.

Then, later, the uneasy, but shrewd, reply of Lord Fitzjames the Lord Chief justice to Lord Chancellor Audley:

> I must confess that if the Act of Parliament be not unlawful, then is not the Indictment in my conscience insufficient.

Finally those last words, words which even those venal Commissioners appointed to try him can surely never have forgotten — those Commissioners whose names sound like the roll of English chivalry called by Henry V upon the eve of Agincourt only *they* were a roll of honour and not, as here, a roll of infamy: Lord Chancellor Audley; the Dukes of Norfolk and Suffolk; the Earls of Huntingdonshire, of Cumberland, of Wiltshire; Lords Montague, Rochford and Windsor; the two Chief Justices; the Judges; and Thomas Cromwell.

These were the Commissioners who two weeks earlier had condemned John Fisher, and among whom were numbered the father, uncle and brother of Anne Boleyn whose Coronation the prisoner had so demonstratively ignored. And those final words, which they heard from More, will surely forever haunt the stones and beams of Westminster Hall:

> So I verily trust and shall therefore right heartily pray, that tho' your Lordships have here in earth been judges to my condemnation, we may yet hereafter in heaven merrily all meet together to our lasting salvation.

As I stood there in that mysterious place amid the dark shadows cast by the twentieth century lights in that dramatic hall, through which twentieth century Ministers and MPs daily pass, I could imagine the bent, bearded frail figure, moving slowly and courteously out to the river, the Tower, and to martyrdom. Perhaps that worldly Duke of Norfolk, when he lay some twelve years later a prisoner in the Tower (doubtless praying for, and being granted, unworthily, the death of the King) he remembered the 'Parish Clerk' Lord Chancellor, and understood what Thomas More sought to teach to all public men then and thereafter — that a Power exists superior to the State they serve.

74

Those words I have repeated this evening are well-known to all of you. But they can never be repeated too often. They epitomise the public man of whose public life I speak today. For Thomas More is the especial Saint, not only of all Englishmen and of all lawyers, but of all public men whose lives take them into the service of the State. But you must forgive a particle of chauvinistic pride, when I emphasise that he was, in essence, the most English of men who ever played a major part in the public affairs of our Nation.

What then does he teach us, his disciples and his followers? To some, public service is a desire and a need — a fulfilment, the only fulfilment of restless ambition and spirit. It is, however, a worthy and honourable pursuit, that of the leadership of the community in which a man lives. To others, public service is a duty, a hard duty that everyone, in any society, must for some part of their lives perform if they are to justify the reason for their lives.

Certainly in the 16th century, and for long thereafter, public service brought with it the chances of truly glittering prizes: position, title, wealth, land. But with the prizes went the attendant risks of abrupt turns in the wheel of fortune. In place of banqueting hall and musicians gallery came, very swiftly, the stench of imprisonment in the Tower, the scaffold, or worse: Tyburn Tree.

Nowadays the circumstances of public life are obviously very different in form and degree, at least in what remains of free Christendom and the Great Republic across the Atlantic. Yet even in those societies the shifts of fortune can still today be abrupt.

Even the greatest in position can, in so short a time, find themselves wandering along a Californian beach, dishonoured and despised, close servants or ministers, in prison — although, apparently, awaiting a rich reward in royalties, and books, and fees for cosy chats on television! Such are the *mores* of today. In totalitarian countries, the consequences of a fall more closely resemble the 16th century.

Whatever the rewards of public life, the dangers and hardships remain, even today, even in the Western World. How easy, then, the role of author or even of a literary or political or religious controversialist, snug in his library or in his study. Not for him personal, physical confrontation. Not for him, nowadays, even the contest of the modern hustings. Rarely will he receive abuse from fellow commentators, and certainly no physical insult. For that is ever the more comfortable, more safe role, — the role enjoyed by the Observer, or the armchair critic throughout the ages. Not for him discomfort, not for him danger. Not for him exposure to all the direct temptations of power, that most insidious of weapons in all the devil's armoury. Some controversialists have power, but it is power without responsibility — 'the prerogative of the harlot throughout the ages'. But to some, who sit or dispute or criticize in the comfort of home or office and never venture into the lists, there perhaps sometimes may come the memory of the parable of the man who buried his talents in the ground: and they may reflect and wonder if their reluctance has come from cowardice, or timidity, or idleness. They are the men who, in every age, turn their backs upon the burdens of public duty and shrink from the rigours of effort and responsibility in public service. As Edmund Burke said: 'All that is necessary for the triumph of evil is that good men do nothing'.

What in modern times is true was much more true in the 16th century, when the temptation to shrink from the real terrors and dangers of public service was far greater. How easy, how attractive, to settle for the life of historian, of academic, safe, surrounded by friends and family, discussing and disputing and composing, comforted, of course, by great devotion to religion; but hiding from the gales of the revolutionary 16th century world; feeling, even expressing, sorrow at the new styles; but ultimately accepting the New Order; and so surviving amid the joys of family and bodily comfort and ease!

Or, alternatively, how easy to settle for the mere practitioner of the law, applying, learning, following professional standards with high integrity, and justly applying the statute and the law made by King, Council and Parliament, be it what it may. Although certainly a degree or two more 'public' than the study and the library, yet more tranquil than the terrors and fierceness of the public political forum.

For, in every age, there is a wide distinction between engaging in rational argument, in sensible debate, oral or written, between observers or philosophers of equal intellectual integrity, affording opportunity for the application of learning and scholarship, dealing in controversy conducted in conditions of gentlemanly differences; and participation in the field where men's very lives are the stakes, amid public affairs, ever shifting and changing, managing the others, persuading, cajoling them to follow causes to which few are inclined, but from which, they believe, many will advantage.

The practice of politics, the Art of the possible, is ultimately the most real of all human activities in every age and in every time. And in any age, the most difficult. According to a distinguished modern journalist:

> Politics is not a prize-giving or a garden fête. It is the attempt to reconcile the all too discordant appetites, wills, interests and aspirations of men — whether men in mass or individual men in the closets of power — in no more than the hope that any decision will at least be in the direction of the people's good.

To illustrate what that means, even in modern, respectable times, a modern English Prime Minister, in a speech to the members of the Royal Academy forty years ago, jocularly remarked in comparing the artist with the statesman in the twentieth century:

> Your instruments by which you work are dumb pencils or paints. Ours are neither dumb, nor inert. I often think we rather resemble Alice in Wonderland who tried to play croquet with a flamingo instead of a mallet.

For in great issues of State, again throughout the ages, men who seek to serve the public must always be conscious that the task to which they have set their hands will always be the most dangerous. But if a man like More had in his time played the academic, the pamphleteer, alone, what hope can there ever be for the Good and for the Just ?

One, therefore, of the reasons why Thomas More will always remain the exemplar for all Englishmen who seek public service, is that he forbore his natural inclination and subdued his personal taste to study, to teach, to reflect, to pass his time in agreeable intellectual and spiritual pursuits; and, instead, he chose the heroic path and went out into the storms of the world.

But if he forbore much that his natural inclination led him to, one thing he never ever forbore : and that was to pray. Just because he knew that he must resist the temptation to settle for a life of quiet reflection and give his talents to public work, so he also knew how much that life needed the strength afforded only through prayer — so the singing in the parish choir!

This is one important facet of this remarkable human being that makes him still so relevant, still so immensely relevant, to modern man. For he teaches us all the lesson that, especially in times of great trouble, of present or threatening revolution, no man should flinch from duty to serve.

Before, then, we even contemplate what he taught those who followed him in the public life of England, it is worth studying the mundane and worldly (in the best sense) example that his life affords, of how he bore himself in the world and in the transaction of public business in Council, in embassy, in office.

He certainly taught public men the importance of style and poise, of how to walk with kings and not lose the common touch. He taught the need for good humour even in moments of extreme seriousness, and with that good humour, ease of address, something which after him many an Englishman subsequently has sought — thus in a sense founding a tradition. He taught the importance of facility in debate, upon which the English tradition (with that of law) again has so greatly turned, perhaps overmuch, — so that skill in debate is given too great a significance!

Also, he taught the need for the acceptance of the authority of the State, although we shall come to the limits which his death taught must be imposed upon the authority of any state. So, in this fashion, a gentleman although not noble, he moved among the grandees of the time, among the natural counsellors of a dictator-king, with the ease of a man sure in himself and in the standards he set himself.

How distant it all is to us, and yet how close! The education in manners, affairs, and debate: University, the Inns of Court, Parliament, the Privy Council.... The issues, stakes, and dangers may be dissimilar and were far graver, and yet they mysteriously seem the same. Witness the threat of Christendom: the division of Christendom; the new thinking, which would, by apparently liberating men, enslave them. Is it all so very different from what we in our time have faced and must yet face?

Then, apart from style and manner, the acceptance of the responsibility to exercise power: although power by its nature has to be exercised by some, in itself its possession spells danger even for the righteous. For it enjoys the most terrible and facile influence to corrupt, and not only in its evil demonstrations. A public man must accept the obligation to wield power. But the power to help or favour, to befriend or assist, even to promote what is thought to be good and excellent, can also corrupt. Once exercised, its possession can so easily become enjoyable: its absence would be painful, like withdrawal symptoms during Lent! And with its constant application, so easily marches Pride.

So the Parish Clerk Lord Chancellor tried to teach his contemporaries (with singular lack of success with his ducal critic) of the essential triviality of what the World calls greatness. But that did not mean that Thomas More did not recognise the necessity of men exercising power over others. He showed that the proper use of power required the greatest personal self-discipline. For Thomas More knew the value to men of ceremony. He knew that Caesar was entitled to his eagles, and to his standards, and to his brass trumpets. He recognized that the State, and the officers of the State, must work amid the trappings of greatness — that men need to see that the authority under which they live has the outward representation of power, so that they can the more readily recognize and acknowledge not only what is owed to authority, but also what authority owes to them. Thus the King has his Crown and Sceptre, the Lord Chancellor his Seal and Chain, and the priest his vestments. How foolish it is to deny men these manifestations. How rash of State, or nowadays, alas, Church to refuse man the colour, the music, and the mystery. The 'ceremony that surrounds the King': the ceremony that surrounds the Mass. So Thomas More, as he moved ever higher in the hierarchy of the society in which he lived and worked, accepted this duty, acknowledged this need. And yet, so as ever to be reminded of the triviality of this worldly necessity, he, for himself, wore next to his skin, mentor to any chance of pride, disguised beneath his finery, the bloodstained shirt of hair beneath the velvet robe and golden chain. To any Catholic who, centuries later, vastly more humbly, intensely less wisely, greatly less honourably, without his grace, his courage, his saintliness, treads some of the paths which he trod, he is ever present.

He is the apt example for every public man. But particularly for the Englishman who four hundred years later follows in the professions he practised, because the institutions (what Isaiah Berlin called 'the plinths of civilisation') in England which nourished him, or which he served, remain very much the same. So, as you join your Inn of Court, the face of the Reader is his; as you plead your first case, in Courts of King's Bench or Chancery, the face of the judge is his; as you take your seat in the House of Commons, the face of the Speaker is his; as you swear your oath on joining the Privy Council (an oath now amended for Catholics so that offensive reference to foreign prelates is eliminated) your voice is the voice of him.

He is the example *non-pareil*, the man who demonstrated with his life and his death that no Parliament, no law, no sovereign, no office, no wealth, no position, no title, subverts the prime loyalty to principle , to faith, and to God.

In England, the practise of the law has ever been the honourable pursuit of men whose intellectual and temperamental bent leads them towards public service. Long before the 16th century England put greater store than other parts of Europe upon the pre-eminence of law.

In the eighteenth century, François Marie Arouet (better known as Voltaire) remarked that '...to be free implies being subject to law alone. The English love their law in the same way as a father loves his children because they created it themselves, or are at least under the impression they created it.

The law, which the English loved because they believed they had created it, had not developed very greatly by the 16th century as it did thereafter. But the common law existed. It was a significant and vital influence governing the lives of Tudor Englishmen: save the law of Treason which, as we shall see, was arbitrarily applied by King Council.

We can thank heaven that old Sir John More, and the natural physical inclination of Thomas, led him away from the contemplative life of the religious, and he became the lawyer and not the priest. Thomas More's early skill in debate, his charm (so attractive to the king), his command of language, must have made him into a remarkable advocate.

When he became a judge, as the Lord Chancellor is a judge, he brought to the law that wider Christian compassion that led him into the use, and thus the development, of the new Chancery injunctions, the use of Equity, which means the application of what the judge feels is right and just over the forms and precedents, often over rigid, of the Common Law. Thus his use of injunction to bring judgments into his personal jurisdiction, overriding the jurisdiction of the judges whose objections and claims to apply the law he had to assuage with charm at dinner.

The just judge knew, before the phrase was coined, that 'justice delayed is justice denied'. So he dealt with the accumulations of work, built-up by the preoccupations of the Cardinal of York, Thomas Wolsey, preoccupations with affairs of State to the detriment of humbler people's disputes and troubles. Thomas More became 'the righteous judge, and true friend to the poor'.

In his short Chancellorship, over which hung the threat of the King's Great Matter and the conflict with the Church, it is this emphasis upon the professional as opposed to the political aspects which prevailed. The Lord Chancellor had received the King's promise to be allowed to abstain from close involvement in what had then become the prime, central issue facing the King's Government or Council, in which the Lord Chancellor was the first counsellor. It was now as though he thrust himself into this part of his duties conscious of the conflict, by then much larger than a man's hand, which threatened the realm, and upon which he knew he would eventually have to make his stand.

Lord Chancellor More did not sign the letter of 1530 urging the Pope to declare the marriage of Henry and Catherine void. The Lord Chancellor did introduce to Parliament the King's Great Matter in 1531, but in words and form which could have left the Parliamentarians in little doubt where stood the first subject in the realm.

When the resignation and withdrawal from public service followed in the next year (after the consent of the clergy to the articles before Canterbury depriving it of the power to enact constitutions without the king's consent) there can have been little doubt in his mind of what shortly he would have to face. I cannot believe that when he wrote to Erasmus in June 1532 of his hope to enjoy being freed of public business so that he might have some time to devote to God and himself, he felt he would have much time. If the 'field' had not yet 'been won', he knew the joust was soon to begin.

Thus as the short respite commenced, and the interrogations were imposed upon him, there remained for him as the lawyer and the public man two tasks: *first:* at any trial to demonstrate any distortion of law and justice, and to reveal to those then alive who had ears to hear and opportunity to learn, the tyrannical application of the law of Treason by King and Council as a political exercise by the State of the weapon of judicial murder; *and second:* when the inevitable result had been, however unlawfully, perpetrated to give his testament, and to demonstrate and reveal the real threat to Christendom posed by the king, and the destruction of the admittedly frail, but still subsisting, unity of Christendom under the papacy. More would do this despite the unworthiness of those who so recently had worn the Triple Crown.

Thus, then, he set out to accomplish his final public tasks. First, to show the unlawfulness and distortion of the process under which he was to be condemned. To do this he employed, as he was indeed entitled to do, and as he was indeed well fitted to do, his skills and learning as a lawyer. For he wished to show to the England of his day and the England of tomorrow, what manner of men, what lack of legal principle, what use of tyranny, were being employed against him and others, and against the nation itself.

So, his silence upon the oaths, claiming, justly, that in accordance with the Common Law 'he that holdeth his peace seemeth to consent'. If his judges denied that in the course of any lawful trial, then the law was being aborted. Just as he knew that no defence would be accepted of any claim that no act by him had been 'malicious' (as he correctly advised John Fisher), so he knew that, to condemn him, his judges would be, and must be seen to be, distorting the Common Law of England. Tyranny must not be permitted to disguise itself in law.

So Thomas More, the common lawyer, son of a judge, Bencher of Lincoln's Inn, one time Lord Chancellor, was determined to strip away the pretence of 'justice' as applied to those arraigned for treason because they could not accept the Supremacy.

Law, that of Man as well as that of God, was (as it is today) the fabric of all civilized society. Therefore strip the trial of all Law, and the naked face of royal policy could be seen for what it was.

Thus, he dealt with the first three counts of the indictment. Those he must have anticipated. They concerned his 'silence' and his correspondence in the Tower with his friend, John Fisher, this last so trivial that it was easily swept aside. Fisher was less experienced in the affairs of the world than More, as befitted a bishop compared to a Lord Chancellor. So Fisher's conversation with Chapuys, so bluntly avoided by More; yet Fisher was a man of uncompromising courage whose strength must have sustained More as More's did Fisher.

Then, in the trial, More was confronted with the testimony of Richard Rich, Solicitor General.

When I was Attorney General of England (having some years previously served in the administration of Mr. Harold Macmillan as Solicitor General: the Attorney General is the senior of the two law officers of the Crown) I caused to be sought out a collection either of portraits, prints, or photographs of all the Attorneys and Solicitors General of England since the first record of the offices in the early 14th century. When collected, these portraits were hung upon and lined the corridors of the chambers in the Royal Courts of justice used by the two law officers of the Crown. So when, over some four years, I passed to and fro, I passed between the pictures of my predecessors. Among them were those of Sir Mathew Hales, Attorney General, the Counsel who prosecuted Thomas More, and of Richard Rich who perjured himself and betrayed Thomas More. The face of Rich matched his conduct, and I can say nothing worse about him.

Yet when Rich gave his evidence in support of the fourth and last count, and so 'undid' all that Thomas More had done to rebut the first count, More knew that in the context of this so-called trial all was lost, for technically here was evidence of More's repudiation of the Supremacy. In furtherance of the purpose which he had set himself, namely to reveal the illegality, there only remained the opportunity to demonstrate how false was this alleged testimony and how unworthy it was of credence.

So there followed the cross-examination of Richard Rich, an angry, effective, biting cross-examination of a witness whose testimony Southwell and Palmer refused to corroborate, and which effectively destroyed the credibility of the witness. What then was left of this so-called indictment in this so-called trial? Only the discredited testimony of a sole witness which no doubt, if it were a Court, no Court would ever have accepted. And the final consequence for the Crown (if this had been a valid trial) was great. For the Crown had taken a great risk. It had placed into issue its own credibility, because it had risked producing the testimony of one of its own law officers. If he were discredited, the Crown was discredited. There was, of course, no risk of rejection. The Commission would see to that. There was only risk of discredit, and that was what happened.

Thus Thomas More, lawyer, executed the first of his final purposes. To what end? Little in his lifetime because of the strength of the tyranny: much for posterity.

His second purpose was to show what truly was the King's purpose, and where it must lead, and to give his own testament. For a moment it appeared that no opportunity would be given as Lord Chancellor Audley moved to give judgement. Again the lawyer intervened:

> My Lord, when I was toward the law, [what a wonderful description of More's great career!] the manner in such case was to ask the prisoner before judgement why judgement should not be given against him.

The gentle, but magisterial, rebuke again calling the so-called judges to some form of legal order.

Finally, the great speech expressing the principle of the limits set by divine law, so that should the state trespass beyond those limits, a Christian must put God, conscience and Church first.

Thus he delimited in modern terms, for all times, the duties of the subject or citizen. Thus he demonstrated one king's tyrannical purpose. Thus he showed to all men of his time, and of all time thereafter, the duty a man owes to God, be the temptation of power, position, wealth, family, ease, never so great.

When that frail figure (which I saw in my imagination last Thursday in Westminster Hall) had spoken those last graceful words of forgiveness upon his judges, saluting them with the hope that they would meet merrily in heaven, and turned and left Westminster Hall, he left behind words and a spirit to guide and uplift all who follow in any age in the service of Crown or State.

Sometime, somehow, in matters less immense than those which he had to face, every public man may have to face a similar choice. Then he will have to make his own decision when interest conflicts with principle. The consequences, to history and to his own life will be less great than the consequences to Thomas More. The alternative may or may not be the scaffold, or its modern equivalent. He may or may not have been a First Minister with a name honoured throughout the civilised world. But the decision he faces will be in principle, though not in degree, the same. It may present the alternative between advancement, security, wealth, safety; and demotion, worldly disgrace, poverty, ridicule. It will present the choice between the world and the spirit.

Thomas More was the first in modern times to show the way. He taught us that the State is not all. He taught all men, and public men especially, that be the cost never so dear, that be the consequences to position, ease, wealth, worldly honour, even family, never so great, a man must choose the spirit.

Each man, to be a man, must be God's good servant first, and always.

85

VIII THE COUNTESS OF LONGFORD

Elizabeth Longford was educated at Headington School, Oxford, Lady Margaret Hall, Oxford (M.A.). She was a Trustee of the National Portrait Gallery 1968-78 and was made Hon. D.Litt, Sussex University, 1970 and Hon. Life President of the Women Writers and Journalists 1979. Among her many publications are: The Royal House of Windsor *1974*; Churchill *1974*; Life of Byron *1976*; The Queen Mother — a biography *1981*; Elizabeth R *1983*; The Pebbled Shore *(an autobiography) 1986*; The Oxford Book of Royal Anecdotes *1989.*

When the Reverend Hugh Albin invited me to preach at the 13th Sir Thomas More Service of Commemoration my reactions were, in Winston Churchill's words, grave and gay. Grave, because I would be the first woman to speak in St Dunstan's pulpit, and I could not forget that fifty years earlier, when I preached to a Birmingham congregation I hoped would soon be represented by me in Parliament, the first hymn they chose began with the line 'God send us men...'

At the same time the invitation made me feel cheerful. I longed to see the ancient church with its chapel, containing the 'head' (skull) of St Thomas More. I lived — and still live — in Chelsea, ten minutes' walk from Chelsea Old Church with its More chapel. This was where Thomas worshipped in the sunny days when his friend Henry VIII would come by boat to dine with his Lord Chancellor strolling afterwards in the garden with his arm round Thomas's neck — a neck that he was shortly to consign to the executioner's axe.

Thomas More has always been my favourite saint and when Hugh Albin's invitation arrived I had recently described my allegiance to his memory in an article in *The Times*. I quoted my favourite More story, according to which the two great European scholars, the Catholic More and the Catholic-Humanist Erasmus, met for the first time without recognising each other and at once fell into a fierce theological argument. Suddenly the penny dropped and Erasmus said to his verbal antagonist: *'Aut Morus aut nullus'* — 'You are either More or no one'. To which More replied I imagine with a laugh

'Aut Erasmus aut diabolus' — 'You are either Erasmus or the devil!' After which they became firm friends.

This anecdote seems to me particularly appropriate to the ecumenical aspect of the commemoration in St Dunstan's. Sir Thomas More himself would have loved the idea of ecumenism. In my understanding of the ecumenical spirit, while seeking out the resemblances between all religions those guided by the spirit remain ardent devotees of their own persuasion. This was exactly Thomas More.

It was More's unique combination of wit, literary skill, scholarship, humanity and sanctity that confirmed him as my favourite saint. Meanwhile, in 1982-1983 [the latter year being that of my St Dunstan's visit] two new books were published about More. One attacked his lack of humanity, the other revealed its greatness.

Jasper Ridley was the author of *The Statesman and the Fanatic*, Cardinal Wolsey being the statesman and Thomas More the fanatic. (In the American edition of the book, the title 'Saint' was substituted for 'Fanatic'). Jasper Ridley is a distinguished historian and delightful person, but one must remember that he is related to the Protestant martyr Ridley who was burnt at the stake. Ridley cites against More his cruelty: as Chancellor he ordered five burnings in eight years whereas it is calculated that Wolsey would have ordered only four. Of course More's record was five too many. But he was carrying out the cruel laws of that period against heretics. In a physical sense he treated himself also with a certain degree of harshness, wearing a permanent hair shirt.

A fairly recent exhibition at the National Portrait Gallery dedicated to Thomas More showed that the actual hair shirt, lent by Stonyhurst College for the occasion, was an extremely uncomfortable affair. Jasper Ridley confessed to preferring Wolsey's cynicism to More's fanaticism. 'In the midst of the unparalleled dangers', Ridley wrote, 'which confront mankind in the last quarter of the 20th century, our greatest hope is that our fate will lie in the hands of a modern Wolsey and not of a modern Thomas More.'

I cannot agree. Nor do I think that Wolsey himself would have agreed in the last resort. For we are asked to entrust our future to the type of man who puts God second, rather than to the one who puts God first. Why not compare the famous last words of Wolsey and More? *Wolsey:* 'If I had served God as diligently as I have done the King he would not have given me over in my grey hairs.' *More:* 'I die the King's good servant but God's first.'

The second book published about More was Lady Norrington's *In the Shadow of a Saint,* the story of Dame Alice More, Thomas's second wife. She was practical, loyal and funny, not More's extra hair shirt as legend has sometimes suggested. An argument between Dame Alice and Thomas as to whether or not he should take the Oath of Supremacy and so save or sacrifice his own life, is full of human touches. Suppose he does indeed take the oath, begins Thomas. 'And how long, my Alice, shall I be able to enjoy this life?' 'A full twenty years if God so wills.' 'Do you wish me then to change eternity for twenty years? Nay, good wife you do not bargain very skilfully. If you had said some *thousand* of years you would have said something, but what would even that be in comparison with eternity?'

And so More chose martyrdom: to be a martyr of conscience. It is this that we love and admire in him today and which makes him both a Catholic and Protestant in the truest sense.

Here is a picture of his cell in the Tower of London for those who have not seen it, to give colour to the blacks and greys of tragedy. The cell is in the Bell Tower, a small, grim place, but at least not dark. On a platform in the window embrasure stood his desk for reading. No fireplace, but a brasier that made letter-writing possible during the last bad three weeks; a bed and a privy in the left hand corner towards Traitors' Gate. Through the single slit window a view to Tower Hill, seven minutes' walk away. More could watch the footsteps of other doomed men, pilgrims to a sudden eternity; he was soon to follow in those footsteps. The Governor of the Tower lived in 'Queen's House' that abutted on the Bell Tower, to prevent important prisoners like More from escaping. After the martyrdom he was buried in the Tower church of St Peter's *ad Vincula*, his bones now lying in one of two boxes in the crypt.

Sir Thomas More was of a merry disposition despite everything. Honoured as the 'Laughing Philosopher' and the man who exchanged the noble title of 'Sir' for the nobler one of 'Saint', Thomas More was no sad or solemn wiseacre. Enjoying scholarly jokes with friends like Erasmus and conjugal quips with his wife, he used his family as a sounding-board for trying out playful or ironical ideas in *Utopia*, such as euthanasia and Plato's views on slavery. Laughter was the framework for prayer, so that he and his beloved daughter Margaret Roper and all of us may 'merrily meet in Heaven.'

The Dedication of the Ecumenical Window in 1984. The Vicar (Revd Hugh O. Albin) is beside Archbishop Robert Runcie and the Churchwardens Mr Terence Wright and Dr John James. The artist, John Hayward, is on the extreme right.

IX THE MOST REVEREND AND RIGHT HONOURABLE ROBERT ALEXANDER KENNEDY RUNCIE, D.D.,M.C.,P.C.

FORMERLY LORD ARCHBISHOP OF CANTERBURY, PRIMATE OF ALL ENGLAND AND METROPOLITAN.

Born in 1921, Archbishop Runcie was educated at Merchant Taylors' and Brasenose College, Oxford (M.A. 1948). He became Vice Principal of Westcott House, Cambridge (1954-56) and Fellow, Dean and Assistant Tutor of Trinity Hall, Cambridge (1956-60). He was appointed Vicar of Cuddesdon and Principal of Cuddesdon College in 1960, Bishop of St Albans in 1970 and Archbishop of Canterbury in 1980. The recipient of doctorates from Oxford, Cambridge, Liverpool and The West Indies, he has been Honorary Assistant Bishop of St Albans and a Life Peer since his retirement in 1991.

My text is taken from the words of Our Lord:

> Not everyone who says 'Lord, Lord' shall enter into the Kingdom of Heaven, but he who does the will of my Father in Heaven.

Coming to St Dunstan's tonight in such a company as this is for me a very moving occasion. Here is a holy place. A Church which has atmosphere and remarkable sacred associations. To be sensitive to places and their associations seems to me to be a human thing and I believe that humanity and holiness go together. When Our Lord wept over the temple at Jerusalem, he accepted and blessed our attachment to places. The English poet, Rudyard Kipling, once wrote some memorable lines — 'God gave all man all earth to love but since man's heart is small ordained for each one spot should be beloved over all'.

A place, a Church, a shrine can be a nursery for our affections and for our faith. Here we remember first St Dunstan. Someone deeply rooted in the Benedictine tradition on which Canterbury and the English mission was first established. But Dunstan, who brought shape and order and inspiration to our Church in the tenth century, was no mere ecclesiastic. He is associated with painting and music, bells and metal work. You don't need to take my word for that. I draw that list from the most reliable of sources — *The Oxford Book of Saints*.

Here is a place associated with Thomas More — and this is the reason why we welcome to our worship tonight pilgrims from Germany and the United States whose own Churches are holy places where they cherish the name of a great Englishman who was no mere ecclesiastic but someone who was deeply immersed in, and cared for, the life of the people of this land.

Near to my home in London, looking across the Thames, there is a fine statue of Thomas More. I often pass it in my car and each time I think how much that work of art manages to blend steadfastness and serenity in the sort of way which encourages and fortifies anyone who is called to leadership in the Christian Church. How fitting that his head relic should rest here in St Dunstan's Church.

But places and people are signs, sacraments and symbols. The deeper we depend on them, the more they should point us Gospel Christians forward in our pilgrimage of faith in this world. We are not thinking tonight only about the past but about the word of God for our day and for carrying forward the Christian vision into the future and sharing it in a world characterised by so much violence, division and oppression.

So you have created a window, a picture, a symbol to enrich your Church and to inspire us all. This is a bold and imaginative venture and I would like to tell you why.

'Not everyone who says 'Lord, Lord' shall enter into the Kingdom of Heaven but he who does the will of my Father in Heaven'.

One of our major difficulties in the West today is that words, mere words, won't do on their own for proclaiming the Gospel or making converts. Words have never been more plentiful — in newspapers, radio, TV, advertisements, election addresses, thoughts for the day — and they are sometimes suspect among a people who have been battered by words. Again, many of the verbal languages people speak are so specialised that they only appeal to others in the same group with the result that not only those of different nations but those of different professions, different backgrounds, different generations, cannot understand each other — and, without any evil intent, scientists and politicians, shop stewards and lawyers and theologians are not on speaking terms — i.e. they cannot understand each other's language.

A great effort has been made to make the language spoken in our Churches the greatest possible use to the greatest possible number. To that end the Bible has been translated many times in half a century and the liturgy revised and updated and updated again. All that helps but only up to a point — to the point where words crack and fail and all too little attention has been paid to other forms of language.

In times when words have become threadbare, religious truth confusing, the change and pace of life hectic, its quality soulless — holy places and holy people can speak to us without words. Art, music and liturgy do not have to pack their message into the capsules of ideas. They can also bridge so many gaps — racial gaps, national gaps, class gaps, cultural gaps and generation gaps.

Since we are in the Chapel of St Nicholas, let me give you an example. I know the Church in Italy at Bari where the mortal remains of St Nicholas rest in a Chapel. It is one of the places which sticks firmly in my memory. Some years ago, the Pope and a representative of the Orthodox Church met and prayed in that Church. There is before the Shrine of St Nicholas a flame which burns day and night. It is fed by oil which is poured in from two ends of a lamp. The Pope poured oil from one end and the Orthodox Patriarch from the other. That flame is kept burning as a symbol of unity with oil blessed by Catholic and Orthodox alike.

This is to my mind a symbol more powerful than any words likely to be spoken in that Church. Of course, words are important. Truth is paramount to those who follow a Lord who said 'My word is truth'; and what is the word which we should remember especially at Passiontide? I think of the great high-priestly prayer of Our Lord before He went to the Cross — 'I pray not for the world. I pray for these. I pray that they may be one, Father, as we are one — that the world may believe'.

92

Your window is a window to inspire us into obedience to that prayer. Holiness, steadfast loyalty to truth — these are the necessary foundations for Christian mission but, without a sense of unity in that mission, they can divide by the words which are sometimes generated by such qualities alone.

On the Church's birthday in the upper room at Jerusalem there were given the hallmarks of the Christian Church. They were a group of Christian people living in the past but inspired by the Spirit for the greater works which Our Lord had predicted for his people. Third, they were, as the Scriptures say, all together in one place. So I believe that tradition, inspiration and co-operation are the hallmarks of Christian mission.

Recently I have been travelling in other parts of the world and I hope you will forgive me if I give you some personal illustrations of two places where Christian unity is not a luxury but a necessity.

I have been in Uganda — a country of great beauty, fertility and Christian heroism. But it is a tragic place which has been scarred by terrible human divisions. Yet it is a country of Christians who are called as never before to be united in a way which will transcend the divisions of tribe and region and the past history. It so happens that the leadership of the Anglican and Roman Catholic Churches, is drawn from different tribal and regional groups. Certainly, Christian mission began in that country in a spirit of competition, but it has moved into a sense of co-existence and is beginning to think of more co-operation. Only if that momentum is maintained can there be a sufficient Christian witness there to stand up to any oppressive regime and build a Christian future for that lovely land and courageous people.

Only last week, I returned from the Caribbean. Those islands and countries that board those seas must be amongst the most beautiful places in the world. Indeed there is amongst such, a variety of political regimes and local customs, a whole world in itself. Recently they have become deeply aware that they cannot be isolated from the great issues of our time — peace and war, the gap between the rich and the poor peoples. In a world which seems to be dominated by the giants, it is necessary for pygmies to stand together. In a country like Grenada, the shock of seeing four of the Government shot in cold blood evokes the response — 'We never imagined this could happen here'. Yet here is a place where the percentage of practising Christians must be amongst the highest in world populations. Again and again I was told how much the Church could give in re-building confidence and hope in a place like Grenada — or in other places where human rights are so severely threatened. Furthermore, the growing unity between the Churches is threatened by a sort of commercial evangelism which seeks to divide members of Churches between those who are real Christians and no Christians at all.

Unless the Churches can stand together, both against oppression and the heresy that religion is simply an individual matter and the Church is an invisible body — an opinion of which the New Testament knows nothing — we shall fail in what I believe the Lord is calling Christians to be and to do.

These are the reasons why, for me, the dedication of an ecumenical window is not simply a matter of decoration or the enrichment of an old Church. In our Service tonight and in the wonderful gathering of Christians from distant parts and different traditions we are touching the heart of the Christian Gospel and attempting to respond to the calling of Our Lord to be those who are prepared to face the Cross and its cost in order that we may become Easter people in our world.

Not everyone who says 'Lord, Lord' shall enter into the Kingdom of Heaven. Not everyone who dedicates beautiful windows or cherishes much-loved Churches will enter into the Kingdom of Heaven — only those who do the will of my Father in Heaven.

But the will of the Father is clear in the Lord's great high-priestly prayer. Let us resolve that word and window and witness should all become one as we dedicate ourselves and pray for each other in order that tonight shall live in our memories and also provide momentum and not merely memories for the tasks which we all share wherever we may be called to witness and to worship.

X THE RIGHT HONOURABLE SIR ZELMAN COWEN,
A.K.,G.C.M.G.,G.C.V.O.,Q.C.,D.C.L.

*Born in 1919, Sir Zelman Cowen was educated in Melbourne and
at New and Oriel Colleges, Oxford (B.A. 1939; L.L.M. Melbourne
1942; B.C.L., M.A. 1947; D.C.L. Oxford 1968). He was Called to
the Bar at Gray's Inn (1947) and appointed Q.C. in 1972. From
1951-1966 he was Professor of Public Law and Dean of the Faculty
of Law in the University of Melbourne. Knighted in 1976, he was
appointed Governor General of Australia in 1977 and held this post
until 1982 when he became Provost of Oriel College, Oxford, also
holding the position of Pro Vice-Chancellor of Oxford until his
retirement in 1990. He now lives in Melbourne, Australia.*

It is a great pleasure to come to Canterbury and to speak to
you about Sir Thomas More. Rather more than six years ago
I spoke in Australia at a commemoration of the five
hundredth anniversary of More's birth. Much of what I shall
say to you draws on what I learned about More at that time.
It is not a specialist study, for I do not lay claims to such
scholarship, but I hope that what I have to say may be of
interest.

There is abundant testimony to the world's fascination with
Sir Thomas More. In his lifetime he commanded the
friendship of some of the most distinguished men of his age;
the great humanist Erasmus, eleven years his senior, was his
friend and he saw More as the man closest to him in humour
and aspiration. A letter from Erasmus to Ulrich von Hutten
written in 1519 gives a long and fascinating description and
picture of More at that time. Robert Whittinton, an Oxford
grammarian, wrote of More in 1520 a statement famous in
our day for its concluding words, which provide the title for
Bolt's excellent play. 'More is a man of an angel's wit and
singular learning; I know not his fellow. For where is the
man of that gentleness, lowliness and affability? And, as time
requireth a man of marvellous mirth and pastimes, and
sometimes of a sad gravity: a man for all seasons.' And, just
as he was a man for all seasons, so too he was a man for all
ages. In the eighteenth century there was an authoritative

English judgment that 'he was the person of the greatest virtue these islands ever produced.' In 1935, the year of his canonisation, four hundred years after his death, G.K. Chesterton wrote that 'blessed Thomas More is more important at this moment than at any moment since his death, even perhaps the great moment of his death, but he is not quite so important as he will be in one hundred years'time'. Almost half a century has passed since Chesterton wrote and these words don't seem extravagant: the volume and range of More studies continue to grow. Why is it so? An English reviewer writing some two decades ago says that successive generations have found in his character and writings a particular quality which communicates something of value and importance to them, but also says that it is still hard to define the reason for his continuing authority.

Modern Catholic churchmen have essayed judgments on More. Writing at the time of his belated canonisation in 1935, Father Ronald Knox spoke of the apparent contrast in the life of a man 'whose sympathies clearly belonged to the new order of things, who yet died as a protest on behalf of the old order of things … a man passionately interested in men, allowing for their temperaments and sympathizing with their weakness. Yet a humanist, we see, could also be a man of stern principle'. Knox offers the interesting speculation that if More had died in his bed before the question of Henry VIII's divorce came up, people might have predicted that this Renaissance man, More, who was a critic of the abuses in the church, who was a friend of those continental scholars who in large part made the Reformation, would, had he lived, thrown in his lot with the Reformers, with Cranmer and Cromwell; that perhaps as an old man, he would have contributed to the sonorous language of the Anglican prayer book. They would have been wrong of course; they would have failed to perceive *all* of the *seasons*; and in particular the fact that there was a sticking point, and they would have failed to have understood the very complex character of the man.

In a sense, Erasmus appears to have made this mistake. In a letter written *after* More's death he said: 'Would that More had never meddled with that dangerous business and left the theological cause to the theologian.' That in turn prompts the impatient comment of Huizinga: 'As if More had died for aught, but simply for his conscience.' Thirty years after Father Knox wrote about More, the modern Catholic theologian Hans Küng puzzled his way through the question: how does this man *in* the world, *of* the world, a man of humane and liberal scholarship, a man adept at the practices of state business, a man who collected and enjoyed possessions, a man who loved and was deeply committed to his family, match the description of a Christian saint? Can we envisage a saint *in* the world? Küng's exploration of More's character, history and beliefs leaves him in no doubt that the answer is yes.

I fear that I tread deep water here; questions of religion are raised which I have no real qualification or background to debate save of course that they raise issues of *human* character, belief and values which are comprehensible to non-Christians as to Christians. In his introduction to *A Man For All Seasons*, Robert Bolt asks the question: why take More for his hero? As he says 'I am not a Catholic nor even in the meaningful sense of the word a Christian. So by what right do I appropriate a Christian saint to my purposes? Or to put it the other way, why do I take as my hero a man who brings about his own death because he can't put his hands on an old black book and tell an ordinary lie?'

I fear that I am running too far ahead. No doubt some here know a good deal about More. For others the history may be hazy, even, dare I say it, unknown. So let me spell out some details of his life before I go to the broader matters. I take much of the material for this sketch from an essay by Reynolds. More was the son of a lawyer who became a Judge of the Common pleas; he was born in London in 1478 (as we have decided). He was educated at St Anthony's School and in the household of Cardinal Morton. There followed two years at Oxford to which he went at fourteen. His legal training began in 1494 and he was called to the Bar at Lincoln's Inn in 1501. For a time he was attracted to the contemplative life with the Carthusians, but he concluded that he lacked the vocation. Erasmus wrote that More could not pursue the priesthood because of his inability to shake off his longing for a wife. Maybe that was part of it. He was a humanist, learned in Latin and Greek as well as in the works of the early fathers: among close friends were numbered the great English humanists of his day: John Colet, William Grocin, William Lily, William Latimer and Thomas Linacre. He met Erasmus in 1499 and they became lifelong friends. I have already referred to Erasmus's letter to Ulrich von Hutten in which he portrays More in fascinating detail. There is a passage in this letter which I must quote. More, says Erasmus,

> had devoured classical literature from his earliest years. As a lad he applied himself to the study of Greek literature and philosophy: his father so far from helping him (although he is otherwise a good and sensible man) deprived him of all support in his endeavour, and he was almost regarded as disowned, because he seemed to be deserting his father's studies - the father's profession is English jurisprudence. This profession is quite unconnected with true learning, but in Britain those who have made themselves authorities in it are particularly highly regarded and this is there considered the most suitable road to fame since most of the nobility of that island owe their origin to this branch of study. It is said that no-one can become perfect in it without many years of hard work. So although the young man's mind, born for better things, revolted from it, nevertheless after sampling the scholastic disciplines he worked at the law with such success that none was more gladly consulted by litigants and he made a better living at it than any of those who did nothing else, so quick and powerful was his intellect.

I find that a very disconcerting view of the law and of lawyers. It is fascinating to study the way in which More maintained his position both before and during his trial. He took and took ably the legal points open to him. The sticking point was the oath which, as the assertion of royal authority over the church and the denial of papal authority was, in More's unwavering view, beyond the authority of the parliament. He did not deny the temporal power to pre-scribe the royal succession and to declare the legitimacy of the issue of the marriage of Henry with Anne Boleyn. Moreover, in the maintenance of his position, in refusing to take the oath, he maintained a silence as to the reasons and asserted that he had already suffered penalties for doing so. When at his trial, Thomas Cromwell taxed him with the proposition that his silence confirmed his denial of the king's title, More came back with a lawyer's answer. It is well done in *A Man For All Seasons*. Let me read the passage.

> Cromwell: But, Gentlemen of the Jury ... silence can, according to circumstances, speak. Consider, now, the circumstances of the prisoner's silence. The oath was put to good and faithful subjects up and down the country and they had declared His Grace's Title to be just and good. And when it came to the prisoner he refused. He calls this silence. Yet is there a man in this court, is there a man in this country, who does not *know* Sir Thomas More's opinion of this title? Of course not! But how can that be? Because this silence betokened - nay this silence was - not silence at all but most eloquent denial.
>
> More (with some of the academic's impatience for a shoddy line of reasoning): Not so, Mr. Secretary. The maxim is 'qui tacet consentire'. (Turns to Common man.) The maxim of the law is: (very carefully) 'Silence Gives Consent.' If therefore you wish to construe what my silence betokened you must construe that I consented, not that I denied.
>
> Cromwell: Is that what the world in fact construes from it? Do you pretend that is what you *wish* the world to construe from it?
> More: The world must construe according to its wits. This court must construe according to the law.
> Cromwell: I put it to the Court that the prisoner is perverting the law - making smoky what should be a clear light to discover to the Court his own wrongdoing! (Cromwell's official indignation is slipping into genuine anger and More responds.)
> More: The law is not a 'light' for you or any man to see by; the law is not an instrument of any kind. (To the Foreman: The law is a causeway upon which so long as he keeps to it a citizen may walk safely.)

This is very perceptive writing. But of course, More was convicted. And the Lord Chancellor Audley was proceeding immediately to sentence him when Sir Thomas More said [as related in Reynolds' *The Trial of Sir Thomas More*]

> My lord, when I was toward the law, the manner in such case was to ask the prisoner, before judgment, why judgment should not be given against him.' Whereupon the Lord Chancellor, staying his judgment, wherein he had partly proceeded, demanded of him what he was able to say to the contrary; who in this sort most humbly made answer.

Then in this version we have More's statement.

> Seeing that I see ye are determined to condemn me (God knoweth how) I will now in discharge of my conscience speak my mind plainly and freely touching my Indictment and your Statute, withal.
> And forasmuch as this Indictment is grounded upon an Act of Parliament directly repugnant to the laws of God and his Holy Church, the supreme Government of which, or of any part whereof, may no temporal Prince presume by any law to take upon him, as rightfully belonging to the See of Rome, a spiritual preeminence by the mouth of our Saviour himself, personally present upon earth, only to Peter and his successors, Bishops of the same See, by special prerogative granted; it is therefore in law, amongst Christian men, insufficient to charge any Christian man.

I don't pause to debate this massive proposition and what it says about the divine or the natural law and about the limits of the reach of positive law. More finally stated his position specifically, and for this he was prepared to give up all, including life itself.

I am a lawyer, and many lawyers have a keen interest in Sir Thomas More. I have quoted that odd passage from Erasmus's letter to Ulrich von Hutten in which Erasmus told what he thought of the low intellectual values of legal studies, though they might yield substantial material reward to those who mastered them. More was a successful lawyer, and by all accounts he was a good, expeditious judge and

Lord Chancellor. He was assiduous in his attention to business, and rapidly reduced and overcame the backlog in his court. There was a latter day jingle that went:

> When More some time had Chancellor been
> No more suits did remain
> The like will never more be seen
> Till More be there again.

A modern Law Lord, Lord Russell of Killowen, has spoken of the businesslike qualities of More's administration of the office of Chancellor; he speaks too of his control over vexatious Chancery suits and of his concern to bring legal and equitable remedies into harmony. Where he could not succeed by persuasion, he used the equity power to mitigate the rigour of the Common Law by the issue of the equitable remedy of injunction. Lord Russell relates: 'The judges, or some of them, complained; but More, summoning them to dine with him, convinced them of the propriety of his proceedings.' His (Lord Russell's) judgment of More as a Chancellor is that while his name is not associated with great doctrine or great cases, his claim to high standing in the great office which he held for so short a time, rests upon the discharge of his duties in the disposition of cases, humanely, expeditiously and fairly.

More undoubtedly had a clear understanding of the importance of the law. A man was entitled to the protection of the law; he could derive much support and security from the rules and procedures of the law. A man's claim to the protection of the law did not rest upon his merits as a person, on high moral notions of right and wrong, but upon the *legal* validity of his claim. As he said to his son-in-law: 'I assure thee on my faith, that if the parties will at my hands call for justice, then, all were it my father stood on the one side, and the Devil on the other, his cause being good the Devil should have right.' In the passage which I read earlier from the trial in *A Man For All Seasons* there is a good picture of More's attitude to the law. In another passage in the play, Bolt develops the point. It comes earlier, while More is still Chancellor and he has spoken with the slippery

Richard Rich. Rich has just left, and More's family express their concern.

Roper: Arrest him.
Alice: Yes!
More: For what?
Alice: He's dangerous!
Roper: For libel; he's a spy.
Alice: He is! Arrest him!
Margaret: Father, that man's bad.
More: There is no law against that.
Roper: There is! God's law!
More: Then God can arrest him.
Roper: Sophistication upon sophistication!
More: No, sheer simplicity. The law, Roper the law. I know
         what's legal not what's right. And I'll stick to what's
         legal.
Roper: Then you set Man's law above God's!
More: No, far below; but let me draw your attention to a fact —
         I'm *not* God. The currents and eddies of right and wrong
         which you find such plain sailing, I can't navigate. I'm no
         voyager. But in the thickets of the law, oh there I'm a
         forester. I doubt if there's a man alive who could follow
         me there, thank God ... *(He says this to himself)*.
Alice: *(exasperated, pointing after Rich)*: While you talk, he's
         gone!
More: And go he should if he was the Devil himself until he
         broke the law!
Roper: So now you'd give the Devil benefit of law?
More: Yes. What would you do? Cut a great road through the
         law to get after the Devil?
Roper: I'd cut down every law in England to do that!
More: *(roused and excited)*: Oh? *(Advances on Roper)*. And
         when the last law was down, and the Devil turned round
         on you - Where would you hide, Roper, the laws being all
         flat? *(Leaves him)*. This country's planted thick with laws
         from coast to coast — Man's laws, not God's — and if
         you cut them down — and you're just the man to do it —
         d'you really think you could stand upright in the winds
         that would blow then? *(Quietly)* Yes, I'd give the Devil
         benefit of law, for my own safety's sake.

Roper: I have long suspected this; this is the golden calf; the law's your god.

More: *(wearily)*: Oh, Roper, you're a fool, God's my god...

It is a fine passage, in its perception and its understanding, and it bears a great deal of thinking about. I'm sure that it gives a key to the understanding of More and this I believe, he derived from the study, practice and understanding of what Erasmus called English jurisprudence. More understood the importance of the law and its procedures as a protection of the individual; he saw the dangers of playing fast and loose with it. At the end, however, he asserted limits to the reach of the law, and accepted the dire consequence. In all of this, we see not only the problems which confronted More in his time, but great problems which face men in all times.

More's fame rests upon many aspects of his life and activities but, as with most great men who possess such a universal appeal, it is not easy to define the reason for his continuing authority. His name is always associated with his book *Utopia* first published in Latin in 1516, and not published in an English translation until 1551, sixteen years after his death. It is a book which has enjoyed great popularity; a recent writer noted that 24 years is the longest interval which has elapsed between editions in one language or another from 1516 to the present day. For whatever reason, it has attracted and stimulated the imagination of large numbers of people; it is quoted at some length by Karl Marx in *Das Kapital*, and its importance has grown far outside the circumstances which originally brought it forth. The Utopian society portrayed by More poses many puzzles: its account of reason and religious tolerance sits oddly with More's own record particularly in his days as Chancellor, as a persecutor of heretics, and with his vitriolic writings in denunciation of heresy, as in the case of his lengthy and protracted attacks on Tyndale. To what extent the Utopian society is a portrayal of More's own thinking about society is un-clear; his main purpose, it is said, in describing an imagined society is to criticize and to draw attention to the imperfections of contemporary society. Even though *Utopia* may not have been More's view of an ideal society, it must represent something of his own likes and dislikes. It has been

103

said that its appeal lies in the fact that it is a never-failing source of romantic aspiration. 'There is something for everyone, Christian or communist, practical or romantic. This universality, coupled with a vigour and verisimilitude only equalled by Swift has ensured for *Utopia* a popularity which can only increase in the future.'

Utopia is certainly his most famous work. He wrote an unfinished *History of King Richard the Third*, about 1513, in English and Latin versions. More was able to draw on the memories and experiences of contemporaries: his view of Richard was the popularly accepted one which Shakespeare adopted and perpetuated, and it has persisted. There was a substantial body of controversial writing; we know that More had a hand in the preparation of King Henry's *Assertio Septem Sacramentorum*, his reply to Luther, which was published in 1521 and for which the Pope bestowed the title of Defender of the Faith on Henry. More was asked by the King to edit it and see it through the press and when Luther replied in scurrilous terms, More answered under the pseudonym of Gulielmus Rosseus — William Ross — in 1523. From that time until he went to the Tower in 1534 his writings were controversial and in English. Some of them are not pleasing or attractive; I have referred to the drawn out controversy with William Tyndale, of which the distinguished English historian of the Reformation, A.G.Dickens, says 'this dreary verbosity, this infrequency of true intellectual and spiritual presentation shows neither disputant at his best.'

This spate of controversial writing ended with More's commitment to the Tower in April 1534, and he remained there for fifteen months until his trial. For the greater part of that time, he was allowed his books, pen, ink and paper and he used them to write works which were primarily devotional. Among these, in the words of Reynolds, 'calm of mind, all passion spent', he produced his finest and most typical work *A Dialogue of Comfort Against Tribulation*.

All of this work, as the contemporary Yale project for the publication of his works shows, reveals a massive volume of writings. I have read but little of them, but I know that contemporary scholarship is making them available with an apparatus of skilled and distinguished scholarship and criticism.

We have to ask, finally, why, five hundred years on, More attracts so much attention and interest. I have already said that it is not easy to say just why it is so; why his praise and his memory grow with succeeding generations. It is not enough to say that he was a capable lawyer and administrator; there were others greater, but less well remembered. Martyrdom by itself is not enough. Scholarship is not enough, though he wrote one of the best of books. His humanity was tempered by a readiness to deal roughly with heresy and that sat ill with the tolerance practised in *Utopia*. That there was something special in him as a man comes clearly through the words of his great contemporary Erasmus and others who knew him. A modern editor of *Utopia* speaks of a characteristic side of his personality as *festivitas*: a sort of cheerful irony in speech and demeanour stemming partly from his disposition and partly from his deep conviction that it is man's duty to live cheerfully and, as far as possible, delightfully. In most things he was a man of profound moderation, and this permeated his enjoyment and perception of the world and of the things of the world. Pervading all was a profound integrity and while he fought with the instruments of the law available to him to protect himself, at the end he stood firm on irreducible principle. It is not really difficult to understand why Robert Bolt took him for his hero. Ultimately the key to his enduring fame and attraction must be found in the *special* qualities of this man as a person and as a writer, as a man in his times and in all times. The understanding of these qualities is still emerging as scholars continue to labour in the vineyards of *Moreana* to give us a better understanding of him, as they have done almost without cease, since he gave up his life.

XI The Reverend Father Brian Byron, s.t.d.

Father Byron was born in Sydney in 1933 and ordained priest for the Archdiocese of Sydney in 1957. He graduated as a Doctor of Theology at the Gregorian University, Rome, in 1966. His thesis, Loyalty in the Spirituality of St Thomas More, *was published in 1972. Father Byrons has also published articles in England, Ireland, France, the United States and Australia. He has served in several parishes in Sydney and in the Seminaries at Manly and Banyo as a lecturer and spiritual director. Father Byron's booklet — A Theology of Eucharistic Sacrifice — published by the Mercier Press in 1974 in the* Theology Today *series, is an important contribution to Ecumenical thought.*

'... it is Saint Thomas' even and the utas[1] of Saint Peter'. On this date, 6th July, in 1535, before nine in the morning, Sir Thomas More was executed by beheading and thereby attained the crown of martyrdom. The event is commemorated in this church of St Dunstan every year, but it is especially appropriate that we mark it this year, 450 years further down the road of history from the days of More. Much has happened in that time. The circumstances of our meeting tonight testify to the changes the human family and the Christian family have gone through in those years. That someone from a land as yet undiscovered in More's time, should address a gathering in Canterbury, points to the sociological changes. That a Roman Catholic priest should be speaking to an audience of Anglicans and Roman Catholics illustrates the evolution of religious history towards convergence and reconciliation.

We are also celebrating the 50th anniversary of the canonization of John Fisher and Thomas More in Rome in 1935. In some of our celebrations, I must confess, John Fisher has hardly rated a mention. Once or twice, in fact, he has been overlooked. Why is it that Thomas More has attracted so much attention, far greater than even John Fisher?

---

1. 'Octave of the feast' — cf. pp 34 & 112.

I have been asked if there is much interest in More in Australia. The question has made me do a little research and even some exploration.

While West Germany has witnessed the phenomenon of the dedication of 25 parishes to our saint since World War II, Australia has also shown quite a remarkable devotion to him with 16 parishes, schools and colleges named after him.

If you come to Australia on a Thomas More itinerary, I suggest you start in Perth. Visit the University College of St Thomas More where the chapel boasts a set of beautiful stained glass windows with, of course, one of More. This college has an excellent collection of Morean memorabilia and also an impressive original bronze bust of More.

South of Perth is the diocese of Bunbury where there are two churches dedicated to More. The older is at a remote place called Nannup — in that part of Australia all the towns have aboriginal names ending in '-up'. Nannup is a typical outback little town. The church is a quaint weatherboard building, the like of which one would never see in Britain. A previous pastor, the late Fr Bert Adderley, was a scholar who delivered several notable addresses about More in Perth. There is a story about him that he once travelled to Moscow during the cold war years. He apparently raised a few eyebrows by doing things frowned on by the KGB. Someone said to him: 'Aren't you afraid of being sent to Siberia? 'Why should I be?', he replied, 'I've been in Nannup for the last eight years!' No doubt Thomas More helped him to retain his sense of humour.

But the main object of your visit to Bunbury diocese will be the Thomas More church on the Margaret River. Tourist coaches now pull in there regularly several times a day. Margaret River is a holiday resort with beaches, glorious limestone caves and vineyards producing excellent wines including one, a world champion.

The new Catholic church has some remarkable features. It was built mostly by the volunteer labour of parishioners out of local material — rammed earth, granite and timber. It is a very large building which can be divided into two areas, church and hall, or opened into a single large church to cater for the influx of holiday crowds. The altar and the baptismal font are pieces of local timber in natural form. There are

107

colourful windows with appropriate attention to the patron saint.

At Margaret River the ecumenical spirit is abroad. When I was there people were still talking about a big funeral of a well-known Anglican. The Anglican church being too small, the funeral was transferred to St Thomas More's Church. Again, the very night I was there a new pastor was installed in the Anglican Church but the social was held afterwards in the new hall section of St Thomas More's.

Time precludes a description of many other fine institutions named in honour of Thomas More in Australia. However, further evidence of More's influence is provided by organizations named after Thomas More. In Sydney there is a large Catholic legal guild, the Thomas More Society. It is very well organized with regular meetings and annual publications. Usually its meetings are devoted to moral and - legal questions, but on special occasions, such as the fifth centenary of More's birth in 1978, several notable papers were devoted to him. A similar but autonomous society has recently been established in the Newcastle district, north of Sydney. The Catholic legal communities in other capital cities do not have such formal organization but they seem to be able to arrange things very efficiently on an *ad hoc* basis when necessary.

Brisbane must be given credit for having a proper St Thomas More Society, by which I mean one devoted to the study of More himself. It meets four times a year to hear papers on some aspect of More's life and thought. Up till now this society has been a maverick group not affiliated with the international body, *Amici Thomae Mori*. However, first steps have recently been taken to bring this about.

There was a great deal of activity in Australia in 1978 to mark the quincentenary of the birth of St Thomas More. There was an impressive series of dinners, speeches, lectures, seminars, radio and television programmes. V.I.P.s such as the Governor General, Sir Zelman Cowen, were actively involved. We arranged for expert overseas speakers to come to Australia, such as Germain Marc'hadour, Fr Bernard Bassett SJ, Sir Peter (now Lord) Rawlinson, and Geoffrey Elton. A wonderful mediaeval concert was held in the magnificent crypt of St Mary's Cathedral, Sydney. An essay competition on More was held for high school students.

Interest in these activities went far beyond the Catholic and Christian community. In Sydney we had a commemorative dinner which was completely booked out. The Anglican Archbishop, Sir Marcus Loane, and his wife attended, as did Cardinal Sir James Freeman. This was remarkable in itself as Archbishop Loane, a man of strong principle, had not been able in conscience to participate in the visit of Pope Paul VI to Sydney in 1971. At the dinner I was sitting next to Mr Justice Murphy who is not a Christian and is now a judge of the High Court. He like many legal people, parliamentarians and academics, some of no religious affiliation, wanted to celebrate the birthday of More because they felt the need of a patron and found inspiration for their vocations in him.

We have also had two successful Thomas More pilgrimages from Australia, one in 1978, the other in this year 1985; they visited Thomas More sites in and around London and, of course, taking in St Dunstan's, Canterbury.

There have been some Australian publications about St Thomas More. Your service sheet mentions my book, *Loyalty in the Spirituality of St Thomas More,* which, by the way, was published by a good Protestant in Holland. Since then there have been other Australian publications, such as Martin Haley's *Thomas More as Poet. A Flori-Legia Moriae: An Anthology of the Poems of Sir Thomas More, some rendered from the Latin, the rest from his English* (Brisbane 1974).

Our 1978 activities gave birth to several publications. The Australian Catholic Truth Society brought out a pamphlet on the life of More. Papers were published in various periodicals. The principal academic publication came from the Sydney Quincentenary Congress: *Thomas More: Essays on the Icon* (ed B. Byron and D. Grace, Dove Communications, Melbourne, 1980). The key-note address at the Thomas More seminar entitled 'Here I sit: Thomas More's Genius for Dialogue', by Germain Marc'hadour, is reproduced in this work as well as articles on More's poetry, his teaching on Gospel poverty, *The Dialogue of Comfort*, etc.

From what I have said it is evident that More's influence in Australia has been considerable. But it is not a unique case. The phenomenon is repeated in New Zealand, Canada, the United States and elsewhere. Whatever the reason for the widespread interest in More, he provides us with issues, ideals, a life-style and principles which challenge us today as much as they did his contemporaries. He remains a man for all seasons.

Thomas More and Ecumenism

The question of ecumenism is one that arises from our joint service this evening. It is a considerable part of my work and is close to the heart of all who feel pain at the divisions brought about during the sixteenth century. Since More is the reason for our meeting tonight, what relevance has he to our quest for Christian unity?

The phrase, 'Thomas More and Ecumenism', might suggest at first blush a candidate for the title of the world's thinnest book! But it has appeared as a title at least twice in the pages of our periodical *Moreana*. The first time was in a discussion over the suggestion that More's skull should be re-located in Westminster Cathedral. The second was a *resumé* of a sermon on the subject of More and ecumenism delivered by Fr James McConica in the Chelsea Old Church on llth July 1982. His main point seems to have been that neither side at the time of the Reformation in the 16th century knew as much about the New Testament as is known today. Recent appreciation of biblical data has defused many of the Reformation issues. There need be no hint, said Fr McConica, of our being disloyal to our heritage to More and Fisher, Cranmer and Ridley, if we are true to our ultimate Christian origins and under the guidance of the Holy Spirit we seek the truth which alone can bring us to a satisfying unity. The men of the 16th century, locked in heated controversy, would probably have envied the calmer atmosphere of our ecumenical age.

These considerations are only generally connected with More. I have often thought that here and there in More's own writings one may find the beginnings of an ecumenical attitude or at least of religious toleration. Certainly in the pre-Reformation work, Utopia, there is a description of a religious diversity and tolerance up to a point. At a time when this was a novel idea, More was at least engaging in an exercise of parallel thinking. On one occasion during his controversies with the Reformers, More suggested the possibility of Christians. and Moslems allowing missionaries to come into each others' territories on an equal and peaceful basis. Another glimpse of ecumenism occurred when More confided to Roper that the time may come when Catholics would be glad to have their churches peacefully and allow the Reformers to have theirs.

But perhaps it is too much to expect that More could say much directly on ecumenism. The times were not right. However his passion for the unity of Christendom and the transcendence of the Church are the very things for which he died. Gratefully the 20th century has witnessed the awareness of the need of Christian unity and many Churches, including the Roman Catholic Church since Vatican Council II, have committed themselves to this cause.

I have been questioned about ecumenism in Australia. We have the usual ecumenical organizations, there are important dialogues, there has been the formation of Colleges of Divinity in Melbourne, Sydney and Brisbane which involves cooperation in theological education. I may mention Anglican—Roman Catholic relations in particular. In most places in Australia they are similar to those here. The ARCIC *Final Report* was followed by very close contacts between the two churches in Melbourne and Brisbane. In Sydney a national committee was set up by both hierarchies to produce a Study Guide to be used by joint groups at the parish level. As a member of this committee I worked harmoniously with Sydney Anglicans and we became warm friends. In my own parish of Gladesville three joint groups of parishioners, both Anglican and Catholic, were formed and completed the programme with reasonable success.

Nevertheless we have to face a fact. The Sydney Anglican Church is very evangelical and may be unique in the Anglican Communion. This provides us all with a challenge. In such areas Reformation principles are most clearly and starkly preserved. Joint statements will not be accepted if they cloud these issues, if they are ambiguous, if they are vague. The solutions such dialogues provide must satisfy any reasonable believer, whether conservative Roman Catholic or evangelical Anglican. ARCIC II has, I believe, a larger representation of evangelical Anglicans, including Bishop Donald Cameron, an auxiliary Bishop from Sydney, a very reasonable man whom I know well and like very much.

I remember the first time I saw the memorial tablet on the floor of this church of St Dunstan, Canterbury. I was surprised at the words, *Ecclesia Anglicana libera sit*. As you know, they are words from the Magna Carta, quoted by More at the end of his trial. The words indicate that the Kingdom of God transcends the secular power.

This day, July 6th 1985, St Thomas' eve and the octave of St Peter, invites us again to examine the links between Canterbury and Rome, between the successor of St Augustine and Beckett, and the successor of Peter and Gregory. May we who are gathered here for this 450th anniversary of More's death, dare to hope that in 50 years' time some speaker, perhaps as yet unborn, may stand on this spot, on this date, 500 years after that death, and be able to take as a *fait accompli* the unity of our Churches? In the meantime, we must be prepared to make sacrifices, maybe not as great as More's, yet what we can, that the sheep and lambs of Christ may form one flock under one Shepherd.

XII THE LATE REVEREND GEOFFREY CURTIS, C.R.

Father Curtis was a Scholar of University College, Oxford (B.A. 1925). He was at Cuddesdon College from 1925 and Vice-Principal of Dorchester Missionary College from 1928-30. A Missioner at Charterhouse and Bermondsey from 1930-31, he became Vice-Principal of Lichfield Theological College (1932-33) before joining the Community of the Resurrection in 1938. He was author of William of Glasshampton, Friar, Monk, Solitary *(1947) and editor of* The Passion and Martyrdom of the Holy English Carthusian Fathers *(1935).*

The words of Jesus in the upper room on the night of his betrayal: *'In the world ye shall have tribulation: but be of good cheer, I have overcome the world.'* John 16.33

Beloved brothers and sisters in Christ, I count it a privilege and joy to be with you tonight, with the commission to commemorate one whom I have long revered and loved, Saint Thomas More. His name grows ever in glory as the knowledge of him and of his historical situation increases: and at the same time grows our sense of his relevance and significance for our own grim and perplexing but rich and stimulating age.

So I start where I come from — London. Not even Dr Johnson was more of a Londoner than St. Thomas. He was born and bred in the heart of the ancient city of London close to the Walbrook, on one side of which, near Cannon Street Station, the Roman invaders had first settled. Here he lived till, ten years before his death, he moved to Chelsea. It was living here in the noisy street of Bucklebury that he first learnt to worship and was taught his faith in the little parish church of St. Stephen, Walbrook. It was here that his daughter Meg, his first-born, and also his other children, first saw the light. It was as under-sheriff, the most responsible magistrate in the city, that he acquired his intimate knowledge of London. He knew all the sorrow, cruelty and suffering hidden behind the impressive facade of the main streets in a warren of lanes full of tippling houses and brothels among the dwellings of the disheartened poor. It was here that, as London never forgot and as Shakespeare records, in the Mayday demonstration mischievously excited among working folk against working immigrants, More by his eloquence first quelled the riot and then obtained pardon for the rioters. This was the London tradition of evil Mayday with which the old play of 'Sir Thomas More' begins. The grievances of the Londoners against the aliens are vividly and sympathetically depicted by the group of dramatists who were its authors. More quiets the rioters, in a scene of three pages extant in what is certainly the handwriting of its author. That author, says R.W. Chambers, is beyond dispute, William Shakespeare (see the essay by R.W. Chambers in his book 'Man's Unconquerable Mind' on 'Shakespeare and the Play of More'). Professor Chambers records the verdict of the distinguished palaeographer, Sir Edward Maunde Thompson, and he himself gives a statement of the literary evidence.

Allow me to quote some words attributed to More when the rioters have asked for the removal of the strangers from the city of London. It came to him as under-sheriff to deal with the demonstrators:

> Grant them removed, and grant that this your noise
> Hath chid down all the majesty of England.
> Imagine that you see the wretched strangers,
> Their babies at their backs and their poor luggage,
> Plodding to the ports and coasts for transportation,
> And that you sit as kings in your desires,
> Authority quite silenced by your brawl
> And you in ruff of your opinions clothed.
> What had you got? I'll tell you. You had taught
> How insolence and strong hand should prevail,
> How Order should be quelled; and by this pattern
> Not one of you should live an aged man;
> For other ruffians, as their fancies wrought,
> With self-same hand, self reasons and self right,
> Would shark on you; and men like ravenous fishes
> Would feed on one another.

The speeches placed in the mouth of More as he argues with the rioters are a most eloquent and impassioned statement of that respect for authority which was the foundation of the political thinking alike of More and of Shakespeare, who learnt more from Thomas More than from any other Englishman.

Yes, it was in dealing with the poor and disturbed and in administering justice in the Poultry, a court near to the present Bank of England, that More learnt most about human nature and became known as the 'friend of the poor'.

But there are also two villages that counted much in the life of Thomas: each was about two to three miles outside the city of London, one to the west, the other to the east. You know the name of the one to the west — Chelsea. There, ten years before his death, the Chancellor and his second wife, Alice, established their beautiful home. You have glimpses of it in the beautiful picture of More and his family by Holbein. On the other hand few know or think about Thomas' connection with Stepney, the one to the east. But it counted for much. John Colet, More's friend and spiritual director, lived there all his life, first in the house of his father, Sir Henry Colet, then in the rectory: finally, though he had become Dean of St. Paul's Cathedral, in the house at Stepney where he established his mother. Colet was not only a very great preacher and one who taught men how to read the Bible when the Bible was a closed book: besides founding the school of St. Paul, he showed two great men their vocation. Erasmus learnt from him that he was to give his great gifts to bringing before men the New Testament in its original tongue. Thomas More was made to realise that for him, to seek the monastic life would be a way of escape. He was to serve God in the world and exercise his great gifts within it. John Colet and Erasmus came on pilgrimage together to Canterbury, and coming from a church of St. Dunstan's will certainly have prayed in this church. Thomas More was often with them in Stepney where these three friends together will have conferred on how the wounds of the Church could be healed, before praying together in that larger but not so ancient church of St. Dunstan. If all had gone well, if King Henry VIII had not confused the guidance of his conscience with his amorous propensities, there might have issued from Stepney, four and a half centuries ago, that truly catholic reformation which has now begun, the launching of which centuries of sterilising disaster-breeding disunion have delayed.

Colet died too soon to know that these hopes were suffering shipwreck. Thomas and Erasmus had learnt much from Colet, especially that 'it is more important to love God than to know about him'. But More learnt elsewhere the deepest lessons of holiness. No doubt he learnt much from his godly parents, from a priest of his parish church (St. Stephen Walbrook, now most appropriately the headquarters of the Samaritans) from the Archbishop of Canterbury, Cardinal Morton, in whose household Sir John More placed him as page, from his two years in Canterbury College, Oxford, and from his years in London as student of the Law. But his greatest spiritual debt was to another home which he made his own for four years in his early youth when studying the Law. This was the London Charterhouse, a monastery dedicated to silence and solitude, just outside the city walls. Barbara Ward, a well-known economist of international distinction, has recorded her judgment that the years spent at the Charterhouse are needed to explain the strength, the integrity, the heroic single-mindedness of his life.

Many years later, the monks of the Charterhouse were together to face the same ordeal as St. Thomas faced in loneliness. At the Mass in which they sought the guidance of the Holy Spirit as to whether or not to take the oath accepting the King's headship of the Church, there was recorded the phenomena of a Pentecostal kind which inspired the monks to resist unto death. They had with them the Priors of two distant Carthusian monasteries. One was from Epworth in Lincolnshire, a village made famous later by John Wesley and his family. The monks refused the oath and were sent to the Tower. There they received all kinds of excruciating treatment but, thank God, they stood their ground. So one day when Meg Roper was visiting her father, St. Thomas More, a prisoner in the Tower, both looked out of the window and saw the monks setting out on their terrible journey, that is to say to be dragged on hurdles to the gallows at Tyburn, now Marble Arch. 'Dost thou not see, Meg,' said he, 'how these blessed Fathers be cheerfully going to their deaths as bridegrooms go to their marriage.' He went on, 'What a great difference there is between such

116

as have spent all their days in a straight, hard, penitential and painful life and such as have in this world, as thy poor father has, consumed their time in pleasure.' Was there any difference in the eyes of the Lord Jesus Christ? To the ordinary observer the difference would have seemed striking.

Sir Thomas More was specially noted for his perpetual merriment, his irrepressible humour, his caustic irony, his faculty for enjoyment, his love of life in all its variety, his generous self-forgetful friendship and his consequent winning charm. Christian life for him was a celebration, and you will remember how he continued to make merry to the end. On the brink of his being beheaded, 'Come, lieutenant,' he said, when they reached the scaffold, 'this platform is a bit shaky. Help me up and I will look after myself coming down.' When the executioner asked pardon for what he was about to do More says, putting his arm around him, 'You could do me no greater kindness.' And then, 'Cheer up, dear fellow, don't be afraid to do your duty. My neck is very short, so be careful to keep up your reputation.' And then there was that last jest — laying his head on the block: 'Stop a moment,' he said, 'let me put my beard out of the way. That never committed treason!'

But along with this merriment words the most weighty, the most dignified, the most pregnant ever spoken on the scaffold. He asked those present to bear witness with him that he should now suffer death in and for the faith of the Holy Catholic Church. They would pray for him in this world and he would pray for them elsewhere. He then begged them earnestly to pray for the King, that it might please God to give him good counsel, protesting that he died *'The King's good servant, but God's first'*.

Some years later, from that monastery of Epworth in Lincolnshire, an aged monk wrote to comfort a lady who was troubled by the distressful character of the times. He was none other than Father Bouge who had been Thomas More's parish priest and confessor at St. Stephen's, Walbrook. He describes his penitent, the holiest and most selfless layman he had ever known; how, when he left the Charterhouse and with Colet's assistance found marriage was his vocation, his inner life of austerity went on. Thomas continued to get up at two o'clock and work and pray till seven o'clock in the morning. All his life he wore a hairshirt though his wife Alice, discovering this, had begged Father Bouge to advise him against it. Father Bouge knew that there was a close similarity even of ascetic method between the inner life of Thomas and that of the monks from whom in youth he had learnt so much. He also knew, doubtless, as we know, that given the same holy, loving intention and the same faithfulness, all service ranks the same with God.

The buildings of the London Charterhouse were converted by an Elizabethan coal merchant into a unique institution where a school, an almshouse and a chapel stood side by side. Early in the 18th century there came to the school a boy from that Lincolnshire village, whose name was John Wesley. He suffered for his faith. If the Church had kept its freedom and held King Henry VIII at bay, as it would have done if all its leaders had been as faithful as More, St. John Fisher and the monks of the Charterhouse, we should have had in England a Church with imagination large enough to find room for the Wesleys and their great mission, as in earlier days the Church had accepted St. Francis of Assisi and St. Ignatius Loyola and their followers. There is a kinship between Catholicism and Wesleyanism because, like Thomas More, John Wesley gave God priority over the state and its minions. The 18th century bishops, refusing Wesley's demand to provide a ministry for Christians in America, were simply pawns of the establishment, as Thomas Cromwell and his fellows had been of the King. But it is a more evident truth that Protestantism is self-divisive: a truth that has proved itself, since the division of the people of God began, by the still unhealed estrangement between God's older Israel and that Jewish minority who with them convert proselytes.

The wonderful mingling of humour and gravity which is, as I have said, the hallmark of Christian sanctity continues in More to the end. It will afford a classic example of this compound when we are given what is long overdue, a theology of humour. More justified his intermingling of jokes with serious business by pointing out that it is only by the addition of something agreeable and tasty to their fare that the invalids can be induced to take any nourishment at all.

But there is also clearly something deeper — the fact that for him life was celebration. The words of the Lord remain true: 'Be of good cheer; I have overcome the world.' All that makes for misery and disunion and hatred in the world has been overcome upon the Cross. It is in this key that we are to live and bear witness to the Gospel of the crucified but victorious Saviour, the 'young prince of love'.

Father Basset S.J., writes in his book *Born for Friendship*: 'While we must admire his defence both of the Church and the papacy, secretly we may regret that More appeared to die for a partisan issue when in fact he laid down his life for justice, honour and sanity. Our desperate efforts today to achieve some sort of unity between Christians, our legacy of bigotry and bitterness, show us clearly all that More hoped to arrest. In the same way the growth of modern States, bolstered by national pride and professional armies, gave Europe four centuries of useless savage intermittent war.'

Prayer, loving converse with God, was the secret of the strength of Thomas More. This harmonised and intensified all his gifts and insights. The sense of justice which condemned the encroachment of rich landowners, even monastic ones, at the expense of the poor: the English patriotism he strives to combine with a warm European patriotism: his deep interest in the discovery of the new world: his gift as a peacemaker: his eagerness for the promotion of the new learning: his integrity as councillor: his eloquence as advocate: the 'radiant adequacy' of his self-bestowal as friend: his influence over the King: his diligence and faithfulness as father: his wise, tender control of his large family and household — that varied but marvellously united fellowship of love which was his deepest concern and joy: his foresight as statesman: his reverence for authority; — all that so deeply influenced that other great Englishman, Shakespeare, to the extent of making him contribute the crucial part of the play on Thomas More in the reign of Anne Boleyn's daughter, Elizabeth, when it indeed needed courage to praise one who had refused to attend her mother's coronation.

Prayer, in fact, which is faith working by love, was the source of his love of God and all that is his. It gave him a longing for unity, peace, justice and truth. It gave him that wonderful mingling of humour and gravity which is the hall-mark of Christian holiness. It gave him a vivid sense of the communion of saints: a deep realisation of the vital necessity of authority: for prayer is loving obedience. May Saint Thomas More pray for us who seek to recover the unity he prized and who acknowledge the legacy of bigotry and bitter-ness due to the rejection of the light he followed: that we may share his confidence that 'the day is won', that the triumph of love has been achieved by the Lord on Calvary; above all, that we may share the joyous courage which Thomas shared with him who said on the night that he was betrayed, 'Be of good cheer: I have overcome the world'.

And in the words of Saint Thomas's own prayer:

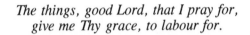

The things, good Lord, that I pray for,
give me Thy grace, to labour for.

Close-up view of the grill and niche showing the hole in the casket which contains the head or skull of Thomas More. The photograph was taken from the interior of the vault.

XIII Mr Tim Tatton-Brown

Tim Tatton-Brown is an architectural historian and archaeologist who carried out the investigation of the Roper Vault in 1978. Born in Nairobi, Kenya, he went to school in Kent and graduated from the Institute of Archaeology in London. He worked extensively throughout the Mediterranean countries before returning to Kent to take up the Directorship of the Canterbury Archaeological Trust in 1975. Now a freelance archaeologist working widely throughout Kent, he is also the mediaeval historian consultant for the Diocese of Canterbury and, as such, advises on the restoration of churches throughout the Diocese, as well as being the consultant for the Cathedrals of Rochester and Chichester.

More was executed on 6th July, 1535 — on the eve of the feast of St Thomas of Canterbury — and, as far as we know, he had no association at all with Canterbury. However, as a young man he was a member of the household of Cardinal Morton, (Archbishop of Canterbury from 1486 to 1500) and must have visited the city and its famous cathedral and shrine of St Thomas. These visits were clearly not at the same time as the well-known 'pilgrimage' of his friend Erasmus, since he would not have agreed with all that Erasmus wrote about the shrine.

In the summer of 1533 More met Elizabeth Barton, 'the Nun of Kent', in the chapel of the monastery of Sion (near Brentford), and was very careful what he said to her. Nevertheless, he was not guarded enough and when she and her associates were convicted of high treason in 1534 he and his friend, Bishop John Fisher (of Rochester) were implicated. After writing to the king and Thomas Cromwell, (he called Elizabeth Barton 'the wicked woman of Canterbury' in his letter to the latter) he was pardoned. Dr. Edward Bocking, the cellarer of Christ Church, Canterbury and Father Resby, a Canterbury Friar Observant (Greyfriar) were not so fortunate. They were convicted of treason and executed after they had recanted at St Paul's Cross in London.

At the time of Thomas More's execution in the summer of 1535 the religious establishments in Canterbury must have been in a very uneasy state. The 'Valor Ecclesiasticus' (a valuation of all the ecclesiastical houses in England) was being carried out, and Dr. Layton, one of the Commissioners appointed 'to inquire into the conditions of religious houses south of the Trent', was staying at the Prior's new lodging, (called the King's Lodging) at Christchurch Priory. While he was staying there, the building was gutted by fire in the middle of the night, and at one point it was thought that the Cathedral might catch fire as well. In a letter written to Thomas Cromwell soon afterwards, Layton tells how he 'sent for the abbot of St Augustine's to be there with me in readiness to have taken down the shrine (of St Thomas), and to send all the jewels to St Augustine's.' In the event, the cathedral came to no harm, but only three years later both St Augustine's Abbey and the shrine of Thomas were being officially demolished.

Over a year earlier the first religious houses in Canterbury had been dissolved. On February 23rd, 1537, St Gregory's Priory, (now being excavated in Northgate) and St Sepulchre's Nunnery were suppressed, and most of the Canons and Nuns pensioned off. The last prioress of St Sepulchre's, Dame Phillipa John, clearly held similar views to Thomas More on the question of the royal supremacy, though she was not brave enough to express them at the time. In her will, written in 1542, she called Henry VIII 'Supreme Head in Hell, (this crossed out), earth, next under GOD, of the church of England and Ireland'.

Within only seven years of the accession of Thomas Cranmer as Archbishop in 1533 (and five years after the execution of Thomas More) Canterbury was turned upside down. All its religious houses had been dissolved and were being demolished and, worse still for the city, the 'pilgrimage business' associated with the shrine of St Thomas had been destroyed. Since that time, Canterbury has been only a minor city — the market town of East Kent — unlike in the Middle Ages, and if it had not been for the emigration of the 'strangers' (Walloons et cetera) over the next few decades, it would have been in a very poor state economically by the end of the sixteenth century.

But what about Sir Thomas More's connection with Canterbury? Why is his head in the burial vault beneath the Roper Chantry chapel in St Dunstan's Church? These are questions that I was asked to address by the last vicar of St Dunstan's, the Reverend Hugh Albin, exactly 11 years ago in 1978, when the 500th anniversary of the birth of Sir Thomas More was being celebrated.

At the end of June of that year, I was approached by Hugh Albin and told that a faculty had been obtained to open the vault and that this was to be undertaken by the church architect, Mr. Peter Marsh and his (then) assistant Henk Strik. I was asked to advise on this work, (particularly as to the recording of it) and for just over a week (from Saturday, 15th July to Monday, 24th July) members of the Canterbury Archaeological Trust, together with Peter Marsh, Henk Strik and Terence Wright (your churchwarden) cleaned out the vault, took photographs, and made detailed drawings of it. Subsequently, I spent some time examining known records relating to the vault, so that its history could be ascertained and, if possible, we could find out when and how Sir Thomas More's skull (head) arrived there.

The story starts with the Roper family who had been resident in Canterbury since at least the thirteenth century, and who by the late fourteenth century were prominent citizens. In 1402 Ralph Roper and his son Edmund and John Rolling founded and built a new chantry chapel of St Nicholas on the south side of the chancel of St Dunstan's Church, and during the next century or so the Roper family, who lived in a large house just down the street from the church, were buried there. The house disappeared two centuries ago, but its entry is still marked by a fine brick gateway with a stepped-gable top, (at last being restored by Canterbury City Council after many years of neglect).

By the beginning of the sixteenth century John Roper, 'sometime General Attorney to our Sovereign Lord King Henry 8', as his memorial said, was head of the family. His principal seat was at Well Hall near Eltham Palace in north-west Kent (now S.E. London) but he also kept his Canterbury house and a house at Chestfield (near Herne Bay) and a London residence as well as owning many manors and properties in Kent. When he died in 1524, his will was so long and complicated that it needed a private Act of Parliament, five years later, to sort it out. Archbishop Warham and Cardinal Wolsey even corresponded about it! This John Roper probably rebuilt the chantry chapel in its present form with brick outer walls, and it is almost certain that it is he, (with his wife Jane) who were commemorated on the (Bethersden marble) tomb at the east end of the south wall of the chantry chapel. The brasses were stolen from the back of all the tombs here in the seventeenth century, but luckily the inscriptions on them were recorded by William Somner.

John's eldest son was William, and as a young man he entered Thomas More's famous household in Chelsea. In 1521 he married More's eldest, (and favourite) daughter Margaret and, in due course, he was to be More's first biographer. This biography which was written soon after More's death but not published until 1626 in Paris, is one of the 'first classics' of modern biography according to one distinguished modern historian.

When Sir Thomas More was at the height of his power and just about to resign the chancellorship in 1532 he composed his own epitaph (and sent a copy to Erasmus for comment) for his proposed monument and burial place in Chelsea Parish Church (now Chelsea Old Church). His hopes for a peaceful retirement were, however, not to come to fruition and, as is well-known, he was executed only three years later for refusing to accept the Royal Supremacy (High Treason). After being beheaded, his body was hurriedly buried in the church of St Peter *ad vincula* in the Tower of London, and his head was parboiled and then put on to the pole on London Bridge that had just held the head of his friend John Fisher. A short time later, we are told, it was acquired by Margaret Roper and she kept it in a box for the rest of her short life*. When she died in 1544 she was buried in Chelsea Church and More's head was presumably put in the vault with her. Her husband, William, lived on as a distinguished lawyer through many troubled years and did not die until he was over 80. He was buried in January, 1578, in the Roper chapel, (now no longer a chantry), in St Dunstan's, and William Somner again records the memorial that stated that he was buried here with Margaret. It seems very likely that her body was removed at this time from Chelsea to Canterbury, (presumably along with More's head), so that it was only in 1578 (coincidentally the centenary year of Thomas More's birth) that his head was brought here, presumably in secret. The removal of bodies (coffins) was more common at that time than today, and though there is no official record of the removal of Margaret, it seems to fit the known facts best.

William Roper's eldest son was Thomas Roper, (his fulsome memorial is on the north side of the chancel, though only moved there from the Chantry Chapel about a century ago) and it was probably Thomas, who died in 1598, who had the present enlarged brick burial vault built. At the north end of the vault a special niche was created, and in it was put the head of Sir Thomas in its lead case. It is behind an iron grill, and has apparently been here ever since, 'keeping watch' over all the coffins in the vault of the later Ropers and Henshaws who succeeded the Ropers in the early eighteenth century. The last burial in the vault, according to the parish registers, was in 1741. In 1837 the vault was opened and the head was seen (an account of this was given in the *Gentleman's Magazine*) and in 1880, during the major restoration of the church, much of the vault was filled with rubble (removed by us in 1978!). An organ was placed in the chapel soon afterwards, almost completely blocking it. More and the Ropers were clearly to be forgotten!

In 1932 things changed and, after the organ had gone a new memorial slab was laid over the place where More's head is. This is where our wreath has been laid today. Three years later, on the 400th anniversary of his death, More was canonised by the Pope and a new era dawned.

Over the last fifty years many books and articles have been written about Sir Thomas More. Most are biased in favour of More, (some are too biased and uncritical), while a few of them, like that by Jasper Ridley, consider that he was a brilliant intellectual who became an intolerant fanatic, only redeemed at the eleventh hour 'by a brave if muted stand for his principles which cost him his life'. Whatever we think today, whether we are Protestants or Roman Catholics, we should all agree that he was, in the famous phrase:

'A MAN FOR ALL SEASONS'.

* NOTE: It may reasonably be assumed that Margaret Roper was given permission by the King's Council to keep her father's severed head. This she would keep in a box or chest. There is a tradition that at Margaret's death the head was passed on to her family. See Christopher Hollis in his *St Thomas More* (p.238, quoting Stapleton as the source). The same tradition is mentioned by E.E.Reynolds in a short article called *The Baynards Story* in *Gazette Thomas More No.1* (1979: p.12). Reynolds there mentions that a quotation from *The Universe* of 12th July 1935 gives us the story. As Reynolds says:
'The presumption was that Margaret Roper had left the chest and the head to Lady Elizabeth Bray. The latter was the eldest daughter of William and Margaret Roper, who had married, as her second husband, Sir Edward Bray of Baynard's, Surrey'.

Note also that Lady Ruth Norrington in her book *In the Shadow of a Saint* (p.115) mentions the same tradition, adding that on Elizabeth Bray's death in 1560, More's head was buried in the Roper vault at St Dunstan's, Canterbury. See also my article *The Opening of the Roper Vault* in *Gazette Thomas More No.1* (1979: p.29). [Editor].

St Dunstan's Church, Canterbury, showing the North-West Entrance. The Church was founded by Archbishop Lanfranc in the 11th Century.

XIV MISS ROSEMARY RENDEL

Rosemary Rendel, who lives in London, was a civil servant whose responsibility was the furnishing of Government houses. She had to give up full time work because of family commitments and became a part-time lecturer in the History of Art. Through her lecturing she formed close connections with The Catholic Record Society *of which she was later appointed Secretary. This led to her association with the* Amici Thomae Mori — *the international association — and she became its local United Kingdom Secretary. She now concentrates on listing images of Thomas More, helping to make new 'friends' for him and encouraging ecumenical relations.*

I think it is true that a man may be known through his friends and one of More's most striking characteristics is his gift for drawing friends to himself.

Before looking at his present-day friends, I think it is useful to remind ourselves how his contemporary friends thought of him. Most people know about Erasmus, his scholar friend, and the group of humanist reformers and educationalists of whom Thomas More was the focus and the heart, and all Europe looked to him on that score. But too often, we forget his other friends: the Bishop, John Fisher, (so near here at Rochester), to whom he looked for spiritual guidance and inspiration but who also consulted him; his parish priest, John Lark, who accepted his leadership (rather late, it is true), and followed him in giving up his life. The Carthusians, of course, with whom he lived four years and who gave him steadfastness by going to their martyrdom ahead of him.

And there are the less well-known: the wealthy Italian/London merchant from Lucca, Antonio Bonvisi, who sent him a warm Angora coat when he was in the Tower. Their letters to one another remind us that the reserved, inarticulate Englishman is an invention of the late 19th century, and never existed in any great number. You find the same expressive warmth in John Henry Newman's letters four centuries later. The letters show us that More did not just give friendship, but needed and accepted it himself: he writes that Bonvisi's "sweet friendship" has been a marvellous comfort to him in "this wreck of my fortunes". The letter gives us another aspect: that he moves easily among all levels of income and culture. He says, "you have always had wealth and there has been no return I could make to you and therefore I value even more your great and simple generosity to me", and Bonvisi writes back that "I have learnt so much from you"; yet More can still say to him, "God grant both you and me to set at naught all the riches of this world with all the glory of it, and the pleasure of this life also, for the love and desire of the eternal joy with God the Father and with his only begotten Son and Redeemer Jesus Christ and with the Holy Spirit proceeding from them both. Thus of all friends most trusty, to me most dearly beloved, fare you well". And there are others I haven't time to name. But, above all, there were his contemporaries, the ordinary mass of people, including the apprentices whom he stopped from rioting. And for these ordinary people he was the poor man's friend and the just judge — a reputation that he has kept through four centuries and still has among ordinary people.

And who are his current friends? The *Amici Thomae Mori* — the Friends of Thomas More — was founded as an international Association in 1962 by a French, an English and a Belgian priest. Within a few years it had about 1000 members all over the world. Its Secretary General, Father Germain Marc'hadour, the first founder, runs it from Angers University in France.

Almost the largest group of friends are in Germany, because More's canonisation in 1935 came two years after Hitler came to power and immediately More was seen as the model for the individual against dictatorship, both by Lutheran and Catholic parishes. The other large group is in the U.S.A. where they have concentrated on More's legal career and on his scholarship. The United States Thomas More Society has many lawyers and judges, but also many university academics. Yale University runs the More project, now almost complete, which is the editing and publishing of all More's writings. Canada too has concentrated on lawyers and judges, though the new internationalism of Canadian society provides many friends 'in exile'.

In New Zealand they have made a special contribution of their own because the University of Otago in Dunedin staged, as a first, the play about More by Shakespeare and others. The Australian friends, in 1992, will host and organise the next three-year conference, (one of the activities of the Association) in Sydney, also a first time for them. There is an important group in Japan, chiefly historians, one of whom [Professor Tokio Momma of Kyoto] has just translated Chamber's *Life of More* into Japanese — another first. The only group in South America is in the Argentine and it is interesting that throughout the Falklands War their friendship for the English *Amici* and Thomas More never wavered or altered. In France, the HQ, as it were, the Friends celebrate More's feast day on June 22 in Paris with a Mass sung in English in one of the French churches and follow it by supper and music in the garden of one of the Friends, as might have happened in Chelsea.

There are many other individual members in different countries: in Spain and Portugal, as you would expect; in Scandinavia and Moscow, where you probably would not; a group of students in Poland; a parish in Malaysia who asked that their newly built parish church should be dedicated to Thomas More as diplomat. The former President of Italy, Francesco Cossiga, first learned of More when he came after the last world war for a spell in a London hospital. He was visited by the Anglican and the Catholic chaplains, both of whom talked to him of Thomas More, and he became a Friend for life. These are all what one might call independent Friends who keep in touch with the Association through news and conferences.

What of us in England — More's countrymen? We seem to concentrate on places where we can sense the spirit of More, (as here), or places where he lived and worked or where he suffered as in the Tower. We make pilgrimages to these places and we like to put up his likeness wherever we know he used to be: his own chapel and the statue at Chelsea; the plaque in Westminster Hall; the portrait in Lincoln's Inn. And apart from the hundred Catholic churches dedicated to him in England, (half to him alone, half with other saints), there are traces of him in all sorts of unexpected places... a housing estate in Finchley named after him; a new block of flats, Thomas More Court, in the Wapping Dockland development; a road subway in Abingdon with his portrait painted on the wall to prevent graffiti, (which it has done); and a parish church in East Ilsley on the road to Oxford where there is a stained glass window inserted in 1845 where the inscription names More as 'blessed' (obviously a vicar who was a very early friend of More).

There is I think in England a great body of ordinary people who cherish More's reputation and are his *friends* but emerge only on special occasions. When in 1978 a great four hundred years anniversary exhibition was mounted at the National Portrait Gallery by two eminent friends of More [Professor J.B. Trapp of London and Professor Hubertus Schulte Herbrüggen of Düsseldorf] it had to be extended and people were turned away from the supplementary lectures because there was not even standing room; and it was a scholarly exhibition by no means on a popular level. It was soon after that we learned that More had been given his own commemorative feast day in the Anglican liturgical calendar, today 6th July, the date of his death which, here, you have celebrated for so long.

Last week I heard the annual Thomas More lecture in Chelsea Old Church, given by Professor Christopher Brooke of Cambridge University. And it was typical that Professor Brooke became a Friend of More through another Friend: he told us that he had been a student at Cambridge of that outstanding Professor of Modern History, Dom David Knowles, the Benedictine, who gave him Roper's life of More, which had fascinated him despite its being a tribute to More as saint and martyr. Professor Brooke considered it his most treasured possession among his books. I think he was quite right when he ended by saying that he saw Thomas More as very much more important in the future as a man of reconciliation — whose friendship we can all share — a major ecumenical figure. Thomas More died for the Unity of the Church — the Unity of all Christians — and his integrity, his clarity and his great ability will certainly help us to move forward continually in that direction.

XV THE MOST REVEREND AND RIGHT HONOURABLE ARTHUR MICHAEL RAMSEY, P.C.,D.D.

FORMERLY LORD ARCHBISHOP OF CANTERBURY, PRIMATE OF ALL ENGLAND AND METROPOLITAN.

Born in 1904, Archbishop Ramsey was a Scholar of Magdalene College, Cambridge (BA 1927, MA 1930, BD 1950, Hon DD 1957, Hon DCL Oxon 1960). He was Sub-Warden of Lincoln Theological College from 1930-36; Canon of Durham and Professor of Divinity, University of Durham 1940; Regius Professor of Divinity, University of Cambridge and Fellow of Magdalene College, Cambridge, 1950-52. Consecrated Bishop of Durham in 1952 he was Translated to York in 1956 and to Canterbury in 1961. He resigned in 1974 and was created Lord Ramsey of Canterbury. He died on 23rd April 1988.

In the name of God, Father, Son and Holy Spirit. Amen. The Revelation of St John the Divine, Chapter 22 verses 3-4:

His servants shall serve Him and they shall see His face.

This is a lovely occasion for Canterbury. A window has been designed and executed with great skill and beauty and sensitivity to commemorate Sir Thomas More, and it is the result of the generosity of friends from the church of St Thomas More in Kansas City and friends from the church of Thomas More in Vienna and from the Parish Priest here as a thank offering for his own priesthood. And through this generosity and this skill there has come about a very significant monument to the great cause with which St Dunstan's has, in recent years, been more and more identified, the cause of uniting the gratitude and devotion of Christian people of all allegiances to Almighty God for a very saintly Christian, and in this way Christians of different traditions in this country are being drawn together as are Christians in England and the United States and on the Continent.

Thomas More was statesman, man of letters, philosopher, social reformer, man of prayer, martyr. He gave loyal service to King Henry VIII so long as the King recognized a power greater than that of earthly kings. He was a loyal

131

son of the one Holy Catholic Church of his time, his greatest loyalty was to God and his conscience.

And so, through the years of history, Thomas More came to be loved in many Churches, in many walks of life, and in many phases of religion, political life, social life and culture. Today Roman Catholics honour him, and rightly so, as one of themselves. Other Christians honour him, and inevitably so, for his width of Christian sympathy. Social reformers honour him as a pioneer, scholars and men of letters honour him as one of the greatest among them, and all of us honour a Christian for whom loyalty to God was always the first and the last. And in this way we salute him as a prophet of truth and a prophet of unity: and how he would rejoice at the sight of many Christians here tonight from different traditions and from different lands, not in the honouring of him so much as in the honouring of the glory of Almighty God that was always Thomas More's supreme motive and goal.

When we pray and strive for Christian Unity we remember that the secret of unity is that we become, as Christians, closer to one another only through becoming closer to Our Lord Himself in the way of holiness. In this the example of Thomas More inspires us, and the prayers of Thomas More, can we doubt it, help us on our way.

The window dedicated this evening depicts with wonderful delicacy and sensitivity the different aspects of Thomas More's life and character; and when you look at it at leisure you will quickly grasp its message. In the left hand lower light you see Thomas More as the family man, the man of home. Passing to the right you see him as the scholar amongst his fellow scholars and divines, and passing on you see him as the statesman, the Chancellor, handling with integrity all the great affairs of statecraft. But now we have passed to the upper lights and very striking there is depicted Thomas More serving at the altar of God, so proud and happy to take his place in the Divine Liturgy, God's altar, God's servant, God's glory, and that's a very moving scene. And then one who thus always put God first in his life not surprisingly put God first when the crisis of conscience came, and so the top light on the right depicts the martyrdom. It was a moving scene, I recall it, through Thomas More's friend. It was Tuesday 6th July, 1535 and Thomas

Pope, came early in the morning to the Tower to tell him that he was to die before nine o'clock. 'The King's pleasure is further', said Pope, 'that at your execution you should not use many words'. The walk to the scaffold soon followed and very soon the news of Thomas More's death and the news of his last words with their great message was travelling far and wide. I quote:

> He spoke little before his execution, only he asked the bystanders to pray for him in this world and he would pray for them elsewhere. Then he begged them to pray earnestly for the King, that it might please God to give him good counsel, protesting that he died the King's good servant but God's first.

The King's good servant but God's first — and that is the message which now, through the years, hundreds and thousands of pilgrims to Canterbury will be reading from the lovely window dedicated in this Service tonight, and may the many pilgrims who come and commemorate Thomas More in this lovely window make their own the prayer which he wrote after the death sentence had been passed upon him — the prayer was this:

> *The things Good Lord that I pray for,*
> *give me thy grace to labour for.*

May those words, may that prayer, be written upon all our hearts. In the name of the Father, and of the Son, and of the Holy Spirit. Amen.

Editorial Note:
  The above is a transcript of the address given by Archbishop Ramsey at the Service for the Dedication of a window to commemorate the life of Sir Thomas More and for the Inauguration of the Friends of St Dunstan's, Canterbury, *on Thursday, 14th June, 1973.*

INDEX

Alice, Dame (Middleton) viii, 12, 37, 67, 77, 88, 102, 115, 118
Anouilh, Jean 65
Anselm, St 57-59, 63, 68, 70
Audley, Thomas 50, 74, 84, 100
Augustine of Canterbury, St 18, 45, 56, 112
Augustine of Hippo, St 15
Australia 22, 95, 106-111
Barton, Elizabeth 48, 121
Basset, Bernard 119
Baynard Story, The 126
Becket, Gilbert 62
Becket, St Thomas 17, 35, 39-47, 51, 52, 55,57, 59-65, 67, 68, 71, 112
Benedictine 37, 48, 49, 53, 61, 65, 90, 130
Benson, William 35, 50
Bilney, Thomas 22, 63
Bolt, Robert 30, 52, 95, 97, 101, 105
Bonvisi, Antonio 8, 127, 128
Bourchier, Cardinal Thomas 51, 69
Brooke, C.N.L. 130
Bunyan, John 26, 27
Burke, Edmund 76
Canterbury College 53, 61, 116
Caribbean 93
Carthusians 21, 68, 97, 127
Chambers, R.W. 47, 51, 65, 83, 114
Charing 59
Charles V 60, 62
Chaucer, Geoffrey 35, 67
Chelsea 12, 17, 22, 28, 37, 48, 49, 72, 113, 115, 129
Chelsea Old Church 8, 10, 86, 110, 124, 130
Chesterton, G.K. 22, 29, 96
Christ Church Cathedral 56
Christ Church Priory 122
Churchill, Winston S. 10, 86

Clement, John 57
Clement VII 62
Colet, John 4, 6, 40, 56, 98, 115-117
Colt, Joanna viii, 7
confutation, The 14, 16, 42
conscience 13, 15-18, 23, 24, 29-32, 40, 51, 74, 85, 88, 97, 100, 109, 115, 132
Cranmer, Thomas 46, 48, 50-52, 55, 56, 59, 61, 69, 70, 96, 110, 122
Cromwell, Thomas 23, 44, 49-52, 61, 69, 74, 96, 99, 118, 121, 122
Crosby Hall 7, 8, 12
custom 6, 7, 14, 38
Debellation 63
Denys, St 45
Duggan, Charles 67
Dunstan, St (church) 4, 11, 39, 42, 86, 87, 90, 91, 106, 109, 112, 115, 123, 124, 126, 131, 133
ecumenism 32, 87, 110, 111
education 9, 22, 56, 78, 111
Eliot, T.S. 17, 25, 33, 41, 44, 64, 68
Elphege, St 45, 57, 64, 68
Elton, G.R. 21, 108
Erasmus viii, 4, 5, 7, 9, 11, 12, 20, 39-44, 48, 50, 52, 53, 58, 60, 62, 67, 82, 86, 87, 89, 95-98, 100, 103, 105, 115, 116, 121, 124, 127
Europe/European 11, 12, 43, 61, 80, 86, 119
family 5, 6, 8, 10-12, 14, 21, 22, 25, 44, 76, 85, 89, 97, 102, 106, 115, 116, 119, 123, 126, 127, 132
Field of Cloth of Gold 59, 70
Fish, Simon 38, 67
Fisher, Bp (St) John 16, 17, 21, 23, 36, 52, 56, 63-65, 74, 83, 106, 110, 118, 121, 124, 127
Flanders 8, 11

LIST OF ILLUSTRATIONS

Photographs by courtesy of Arthur Palmer,
Staff Photographer, Kentish Gazette